Alpha Teen—Millennial Parent

Life Skill Essentials to Future Proof Your Screenager

Evelyne Gilles

© Copyright 2022 - All rights reserved.

The content contained within this book may not be reproduced, duplicated or transmitted without direct written permission from the author or the publisher.

Under no circumstances will any blame or legal responsibility be held against the publisher, or author, for any damages, reparation, or monetary loss due to the information contained within this book, either directly or indirectly.

Legal Notice:

This book is copyright protected. It is only for personal use. You cannot amend, distribute, sell, use, quote or paraphrase any part, or the content within this book, without the consent of the author or publisher.

Disclaimer Notice:

Please note the information contained within this document is for educational and entertainment purposes only. All effort has been executed to present accurate, up to date, reliable, complete information. No warranties of any kind are declared or implied. Readers acknowledge that the author is not engaged in the rendering of legal, financial, medical or professional advice. The content within this book has been derived from various sources. Please consult a licensed professional before attempting any techniques outlined in this book.

By reading this document, the reader agrees that under no circumstances is the author responsible for any losses, direct or indirect, that are incurred as a result of the use of the information contained within this document, including, but not limited to, errors, omissions, or inaccuracies.

Table of Contents

INTRODUCTION 1
    STAY CALM AND USE COMMON SENSE 3
        Born Into Technology, Gen Alpha Needs Help to Live Free 5

CHAPTER 1: SURVIVAL BASICS 9
    HOUSEWORK IS THE FOUNDATION OF MASTERING SURVIVAL SKILLS 10
        Conquer the Fear of Frying 11

CHAPTER 2: SMART HOMES MAKE SMART KIDS 15
    SINGLE TASKING IS SMARTER THAN MULTITASKING 18
        Family Meetings Teach Democracy in the Home 19

CHAPTER 3: BE ORGANIZED 21
    GUIDE YOUR TEEN TO "LIVING OUTSIDE" 23
        Good Habits Last a Lifetime 24

CHAPTER 4: INNER BEAUTY 27
    THE ONSET OF PUBERTY SIGNALS MAJOR CHALLENGES AHEAD 29
        Puberty Is a Challenging Time for Self-Image 31

CHAPTER 5: FIRST IMPRESSIONS COUNT 33
    THE WAY YOU DRESS EXPRESSES YOUR PERSONALITY 34
        The Circular Fashion Revolution 35

CHAPTER 6: HEALTHY BODIES, HEALTHY MINDS 37
    ALWAYS BE CONNECTED TO BASICS 37
        Hygiene First and Be Ready for Emergencies 38

CHAPTER 7: THE CYCLE OF LIFE 41
    THE DESTINY OF THE SOUL IS THE COMMON THREAD 42
        Teens and Sex—Drawing the Line Between Normative and Problematic Behavior 44

CHAPTER 8: WORDS MATTER 49
    LISTEN WITH YOUR EYES AND EARS TO SEE CLEARLY 50

Help Your Teen Own the Solution 52

CHAPTER 9: MANAGING YOURSELF **55**

SOCIAL MEDIA CUTS BOTH WAYS IN TEEN FRIENDSHIPS 56
Hobbies, Community Activity, and the Arts Help Unique Skills and Ripples of Friendship 57

CHAPTER 10: THE AUTHENTIC TEEN **59**

COURTESY IS NEVER OUT OF FASHION 60
What About Birth Order and Sibling Rivalry? 60

CHAPTER 11: EMOTIONAL ENERGY **65**

TRANSITION FROM PLAYMATE TO ROLE MODEL 66
Share Family Time and Expose Your Teen to Spirituality 67

CHAPTER 12: FIRST TASTE OF FREEDOM **71**

THE TEMPTATION TO OVERPARENT IS OVERPOWERING 72
You Are the Best Judge of Your Teen's Ability 73

CHAPTER 13: LIFE-SAVING SKILLS **77**

CATCH THEM YOUNG 77
Lifesaving and CPR Are Useful Emergency Rescue Skills 78

CHAPTER 14: LIVING IN AN "ALWAYS ON" WORLD **92**

THE FIRST GENERATION TO BE BORN CONNECTED 93
Opening Doors, Closing Minds 94

CHAPTER 15: CRITICAL THINKING **98**

ENCOURAGE DIVERSITY 99
Treat Play Seriously 99

CHAPTER 16: PROBLEM SOLVING **102**

STOP CHASING RAINBOWS 103
Faster Is Not Necessarily Better 104

CHAPTER 17: GOAL SETTING **108**

OOPS IS THE NEW SMART FOR EARLY TEENS 109
Learning to Fail Is Better Than Failing to Learn 110

CHAPTER 18: TIME MANAGEMENT **112**

ROLE MODEL TIME MANAGEMENT 112
Everyone's Body Clock Works Differently 113

CHAPTER 19: MONEY MATTERS **116**

MONEY IS MOVING FROM DIGITAL TO VIRTUAL FOR TEENS 117
Teach Them How to Use Money to Create Wealth 118

CHAPTER 20: TRANSPORTATION AND TRAVEL **120**

TRAVEL BROADENS THE MIND BUT KILLS THE ENVIRONMENT 121
Augmented Reality Is Changing the Way Travel Is Experienced .. 121

CHAPTER 21: NAVIGATING LIFE **124**

TECHNOLOGY IS YOUR TEENS COMPASS 124
Teach Survival Skills by Disconnecting From the Grid 125

CHAPTER 22: EARNING A LIVING **126**

ROUTINE JOBS COULD BE TAKEN OVER BY ROBOT WORKERS 127
Jobs Currently Considered Irreplaceable in the Knowledge Economy128

CONCLUSION **131**

AN APPEAL TO BUSY PARENTS AND EARLY TEENS 132
Role Model the Values and Behavior You Expect 133

REFERENCES **140**

Introduction

The share of this (Alpha) generation spending at least part of their early formative years in living arrangements that do not include both of their biological parents is higher than any generation observed in the previous century. When you look at a child in this generation you never know what kind of family life they have experienced. –Elwood Carlson, Professor of Sociology, Florida State University

I see this every day in the increasing number of sad, angry, discouraged children that are sent to me for counseling in the oversubscribed secondary school I teach at in London, England, and the young adults I mentor in my life coach practice. I empathize. I too was separated from my biological mother at 12 months and spent the next five years at my grandmother's house. She brought me up as a happy little toddler who loved singing and public speaking. But then life changed when my grandmother fell sick and left for treatment overseas with my father and I was sent to his sister's house. The next six months of my life with my aunt and cousin were miserable. My father, too, became unpredictable and violent when he married again. My stepmother disliked me with a vengeance for being smarter than her own children, a fate my sister and three brothers did not share. Eventually, my father relented and sent me off to school in Paris when I was on the verge of adolescence.

This is where Maddy saw me, took me in her care, gave me love, and affection, and taught me all the life skills I know today. Maddy was a constant in my life even after I moved again to New York to live with another of my father's sisters. I would return to Paris during vacations to spend time with her and she would visit me in New York.

I never experienced kindness and compassion until I met Maddy. I was a sad, lonely, unwanted, and abused child, invisible to the rest of the world. She was an empathetic, influential, and powerful lady adored by everyone in our Paris arrondissement. I watched from a distance the kindness she showed to children and young people around her but never had the courage to approach her. Yet she saw me and observed my unhappiness, my loneliness, and my pain. She shortly took me in her care and gave me the stability to pursue an education, which, as an immigrant, was the only avenue to pull myself up in life. I realized that I had to work ten times smarter to have half a chance at life's opportunities as a person of color.

I entered university in London, England, to be nearer to Maddy, who was now family to me, as she continued to guide me as an older teen and young adult reading for my degree in psychology and a postgraduate degree in education. I chose education as a career because I felt the need to touch the lives of teens who, as I did, would need to be touched by empathy and kindness through the most formative years of life.

This is my story, unlikely though it may seem, and today, as a secondary school teacher, life coach, and millennial, I have often been provoked by the question: "looking back from where you are today, what advice would your millennial self-give your teen self?" At times, I have asked myself this question when trying to be my best empathetic self in managing stressed and anxious teenagers in my classroom. Often though, it would come from an overanxious parent wanting to give their child every opportunity to succeed in life. At first, this question took me back to my own battles with depression and anxiety when as a pre-teen I moved from country to country, the stress of leaving behind familiar neighborhoods, friends, and family and regularly having to make new friends, learn new social behavior while overcoming the stigma of being the "other" while I put down new roots in an extended family. So, I would reply, "Carpe diem—seize the day." Each day brings its own challenges and by mindfully focusing on the present, you avoid living in the past or worrying too much about an uncertain future. What you do today determines your future.

Stay Calm and Use Common Sense

Parenting is a serious business, and many parents may be unprepared for the changes it brings to their Subjective Well-Being (SWB). First-time mothers particularly tend to be over-optimistic and may soon find themselves overburdened with the workload of early childhood. With more working mothers today and paid maternity leave not mandated by Federal law in the US, mothers are having to use childcare within eight to twelve weeks. Compared to the rest of the world (38%), only 8% of US children live with extended families (Pew, 2019).

The positive and negative experiences of bringing up a baby, plus its social and economic impact, influence the decision to have a second child despite the pleas for a little companion as the toddler grows older. Single-child households are growing and are estimated to be around 22% in the US (Pew Research, 2015). At the same time, so are single-parent family units—23% in the US, 7% and growing in the rest of the world.

Left to fend for themselves, parents are overwhelmed by an abundance of advice and guides for bringing up well-behaved, confident, and successful children. Teens struggling with the emotional and physical changes of adolescence too are in no mood to follow their parents' advice. The groundwork for a better relationship between teens and their parents needs to be in place well before their teen begins to seek greater independence and freedom to explore the outside world. The barrier to this really is the parenting style used in the home, over which children have very little influence or control. It entirely depends on the parent as they struggle to cope with career, home, social life, and the education of their child.

Some parents tend to be ostriches—they do not see the need to move beyond their own experiences. These parents can be either over-ambitious or extremely neglectful. Both of these can be damaging to self-esteem because these parents tend to blame their kids. Even if they do learn of a better approach to parenting, their past holds them back from using it. They may justify using reward and punishment to motivate their children on the basis that this is how they themselves were brought up. The lack of trust in this family leads to the teen seeking advice and guidance from their peer group which results in low self-esteem and makes them vulnerable to risky behavior. On the other extreme, the child can become isolated and introverted too due to the parents' focus on academic or sporting excellence.

The jellyfish approach to parenting is the style used by other parents—over-eager to please their children and avoid conflict, they accept their behavior and do not enforce limits. Obesity, for example, could be a consequence for their child due to the lack of control. These children too could have lower self-esteem and happiness levels.

Parents who respect their children and are respected in return and stand firmly with their decisions but take time to explain why are using what is considered to be the best parenting style to support the development of a socially aware, self-confident, and successful young adult. These parents adopt an authoritative style of parenting, also known as panda parenting—guiding and encouraging their children in the right direction while being playful and engaged.

Raising a responsible, resilient, and respectful adult is the ideal desired by most parents and there is no magic bullet to achieving this. It takes patience, a commitment to staying the course, and belief in your child's talent and ability.

Born Into Technology, Gen Alpha Needs Help to Live Free

As a teacher, I see more parents driving their children to be over-competitive at studies or sports than showing them to have fun. This not only deprives teens of the joy of childhood but also leaves them ill-equipped to live as independent young adults. One symptom of this is the desire to enroll children into oversubscribed secondary schools on the assumption that the end product of education is a young adult with the perfect blend of cognitive, social, creative, and practical skills. The unfortunate fact is that we have an education system that is still mired in producing cannon fodder for the assembly lines of the second. The Industrial Revolution is an outdated model that leaves teens and parents with a huge skills gap to fill as the world transitions to the fourth. The industrial revolution, defined by 5G connectivity and the Internet of Things (IoT).

An often-neglected skill that will be needed in this brave new world is curiosity. Margot Machol Bisnow—Author and a former Chief of Staff of the US President's Council of Economic Advisors, interviewed the parents of 70 successful entrepreneurs for her book *Raising an Entrepreneur: How to Help Your Children Achieve Their Dreams* to ask them what skills they taught from an early age. Curiosity was common across all, and it went beyond simply wanting to know, including asking questions, fixing things, figuring out how they work, and trying to make things better. Fixing things around the house improved decision-making and problem-solving skills.

Parents also encouraged learning by playing together, exploring, and having little adventures. Vacationing, while it may seem daunting to attempt with little children, develops their brains too, while it supports education and encourages them to learn. Exposing children to different experiences and people also helps in making them more accepting and tolerant. And boosts confidence by helping overcome fear of the unknown.

The other factor that helped entrepreneurial success by boosting self-confidence and esteem was to show children that you respect their judgment by allowing them to make decisions instead of telling them what to do. This is by smartly questioning them to understand the possible consequences of their actions and risks and trade-offs while being a safety net to cushion their inevitable falls and bounce them back up again.

Parenting Changes the Adult Brain Too

While the zero to three years have received great attention (and deservedly so) as being vital in brain development and cognitive skills, it is only very recently that researchers have explored the significance of the early teen years, from 11-14, in personality development, and the importance of the nuclear family supporting them in these adolescent years. What seems to be happening is that parents who interact, encourage, and play with children during the infant and toddler years tend to become less involved as they grow through the tween years and reach the teens.

By this time, your teen has demonstrated their competence to manage routines and chores and is thus thought to be independent, while you may by now be mid-career and having to focus more on work or occupation and building wealth to support higher education. The lack of family support and interaction can drive teens to greater dependency on modeling behavior to gain the acceptance of their peer group, which can then lead to declining academic performance, joining a gang and antisocial behavior, and alcohol and drug use.

We know a lot about the development of the brain and cognitive skills in children and that knowledge is expanding with new technology such as MRI scanning to map their brains at different stages of development. But recently researchers have begun turning their attention to parents in an attempt to understand if your brain undergoes changes too when you transition to parenting., Research by Ruth Felderman (2014) using a sample of 89 parents found increased activity in the amygdala and hypothalamus, the two regions concerned with emotions and bonding and the system producing the feel-good hormone dopamine. These changes were seen in both parents except that with fathers it was the mentalizing system (feel-good hormone dopamine production) that is more active when the father engages in caregiving activity. Interestingly, in the case of gay dads, both systems—emotional and mentalizing develop equally.

Giving Love and Hope to Desperate Teens Is My Life's Goal

When I think back to my own experience as a child, I believe that my musician father was always on the road and had very little time or even interest to transition to caregiving for me or my four siblings. He was focused on himself and his career and when my mother divorced him, we were literally a millstone around his neck. He passed us all on to his mother (our grandmother) and when she fell sick; we became even more of a problem to him. My being away from the family since being a baby (sent to my grandmother at 12 months) he and I probably bonded the least. And this made me a target for his anger at life in general, which is the only reason I can reasonably attribute to my regular beatings and threats. When he married again, his attitude influenced my stepmother too. It was only after I met Maddy in Paris and she saw me as a child desperately needing help that my life stabilized and I was able to move forward with my education.

My childhood is still my biggest influence on me as a teacher and I always see my pupils as little human beings in need of love and hope rather than vessels to fill with rote learning to pass examinations. I listen carefully to understand them as individuals and support them with empathy and kindness. I appeal to parents to recognize and celebrate the responsibility for role modeling the values, attitudes, and behaviors you wish to see in your future adult offspring, through the process of guiding them in their early teen years.

In this book, I hope you will find the perfect mix of practical knowledge for your teen to live better and the guidance they need to develop into empathetic, self-confident, and sociable young adults better equipped to understand and meet the challenges of their generation. In its pages, you may find some relief and support as you juggle between career, homemaker, and caregiver and your teen finds a useful reference to light up their path to freedom and independence.

Chapter 1:

Survival Basics

If you want children to keep their feet on the ground, put some responsibility on their shoulders. —Abigail Van Buren, aka "Dear Abby"

Working parents are more likely to compensate for the guilt of spending less time with their children by overindulging them, giving in to their every need, and being reluctant to have them help out with household chores. After all, giving your children a better lifestyle is a significant motivator in work life. But when parents do too much, are you harming your children by depriving them of opportunities to learn essential life skills? These are not taught in schools either, so the danger is your teen could grow up to be a self-indulgent and underprepared young adult who has difficulty fitting into society.

On the other hand, the example of a working mother can build confidence and a greater sense of commitment and social awareness in children. Parents who take a realistic view strike a balance by creating opportunities for their teens to learn by doing and being role models of happy and successful parents.

Food skills and cooking rank at the top of the must-have life skills because proper nutrition is the key to physical and mental energy without which maintaining your health can be challenging. The best way to introduce your teen to skills around food and cooking is to involve them while you do the essential tasks such as grocery shopping, menu planning, recipe selection, ingredient preparation, cooking, using the right utensils and appliances, table setting, serving, cleaning up, preserving and repurposing leftovers. When you engage them in this way, learning these essential homemaker skills becomes fun and not a chore. Not to mention that it lightens the burden on you after a hard day's work. This also creates an opportunity to set up a regular routine of spending quality time while catching up on your child's activity in an informal and relaxed setting.

Housework Is the Foundation of Mastering Survival Skills

Is the weekend your regular grocery shopping habit? You would then be checking on your stock of dry foods, vegetables, and protein, in your freezer, refrigerator, and pantry as well as home supplies to make a grocery list. Asking your teen to help is a great way to teach them several useful skills. Firstly, they learn where things are stored, how frequently they need to be bought, the quantities needed for an average home; they get an idea of the quantities that are used and when you discuss the brands and packs they learn about quality and convenience.

Now you might not be able to do this all the time because young teens would normally have packed schedules, but asking for their help once a month is reasonable. Some families practice a monthly restocking of the larder for dry goods, packaged foods, cleaning products, and personal care. If you already practice this routine (and I highly recommend it if you don't), involving your early teen can make it their homemaker training in a fun way. If you also maintain month-end budgeting, let them help you with updating it with utility payments, mortgage or rent, home repairs and maintenance, travel, and savings. This is a good time to look ahead to plan the next month's spending if there are upcoming birthdays, invitations to parties, and other events that need new clothes or buying gifts. Not only can you plan another joint shopping expedition, but you also save yourself the stress of unexpected shopping demands at inconvenient times.

During their teen years, expect regular requests for increases in their weekly or monthly allowance. Some banks have low-fee teen checking accounts with debit cards for withdrawals from as young as 6-8 years. You could check with your bank if they have this service linked to your own account which allows you to transfer money easily and gives you alerts on withdrawals. Mobile banking Apps offer even greater convenience and features such as tracking expenses, budgeting, and bill split. The allowance thus opens the door to teaching teens financial literacy, a subject that no school curriculum teaches but is the basic knowledge for creating wealth.

Conquer the Fear of Frying

Most teens like to try out simple recipes, but not many aspire to be master chefs. It is best to let them develop their skills gradually, starting with something as simple even as popping corn in the microwave. Salads and simple pasta recipes could be useful as basic cooking skills that support the soon-to-be future young adult as they set off for university or their first job away from home. Your task really is to make them feel safe in the kitchen and understand quantities, ingredients, and flavors. All-knowing Google and YouTube videos will be their guide thereafter, with literally millions of recipes for home cooking.

The pandemic boosted the popularity of food delivery apps and Uber Eats and DoorDash grew rapidly to compete with food delivery from established Quick Service Restaurants (QSR) may dramatically change the way the world eats in the future. While food delivery offers convenience, the menus may not offer nutritional balance and parents may now need to remind themselves of balancing the five basic foods–fruits, vegetables, grains, protein, and dairy in setting the right example for teens to follow. The downside of the internet is that it promotes fads and misinformation, and it is difficult to separate the genuine experts from the scammers. Showing teens to remain grounded in healthy food habits will help them when living independently.

It is also important that children learn the basics of safety in using kitchen appliances and safety as early as possible. In the case of a microwave, the basics would include microwave-safe containers, no aluminum or metal containers, overboiling liquids, use of oven gloves because it heats slowly from the bottom, having a safe space ready to place hot containers, and what foods are best for microwave heating versus oven cooking. Air fryers offer healthier oil-free cooking options and are safer for teens to make french fries because deep fryers that use lots of hot oil will always pose a danger to them. Care in switching any appliance on and off, whether electrical or gas, should be a priority from an early age.

Baking can be a fun activity for teens and moms, although you could start even earlier with simple recipes for cookies, cakes, and muffins. Raw cake batter is an irresistible treat for kids.

For teenagers, food is a touchy topic. Successful marketing of fast food, quick service restaurants, and non-alcoholic, ready-to-drink beverages combined with technology-driven sedentary lifestyles have seen a spike in teen obesity Noncommunicable Diseases (NCD) such as diabetes, cardiovascular, and cancers. Some teenagers also resist new food choices to which their palette is unaccustomed. Of course, if you were a smart parent and introduced different textures and flavors when weaning your infant off milk with their first solid foods, and your family enjoys varied cuisines, you may not have this problem. Summer camp is an option for working parents to expose their teenagers to the outdoors, physical activity, as well as a whole new world of interaction. Encouraging your teen to show off their new skills at home would encourage them to expand them further by helping you with meal preparation when possible. Some camps offer the option of kids cooking. GirlGuiding and Scouting are regular activities that teach your teen skills to be self-sufficient and confident while recognizing and rewarding self-development efforts through badges and tiers. Being worldwide organizations through GirlGuiding and Scouting your teen can meet peers and make friends at local, national, and international events and meetings. Family camping trips and self-catering holidays are an option for experimental cooking and teaching your teen basic survival skills, especially if you choose accommodation sans all modern conveniences as learning experiences. If you are not an outdoor type yourself, it helps to combine family vacations with friends who are more adventurous. Having a circle of friends with children of the same age is a boon to parents.

Many of the products that make modern life convenient have an unfortunate effect on the environment. While as a millennial, growing up, or even as an adult, you would be more aware of climate warming, plastic pollution, and water table depletion, these were still viewed as distant threats to your lifestyle. But as we are seeing extreme weather conditions being more frequent and causing devastation on a larger scale across the world, energy challenges, and income inequality, your Gen Alpha teen is set to enter a world in which sustainability is front and center on the global agenda. Including your teen in planning household purchases is as much an educational opportunity and they may surprise you with their knowledge about newer or better products that may be more socially responsible or even less damaging to the environment but are off your radar due to habit purchasing.

Chapter 2:

Smart Homes Make Smart Kids

Don't raise your children to have more than you had, raise them to be more than you were. —Anon

Household chores, unfortunately, are boring but necessary and most adults would be happy to have someone else do them. Witness the innovation of labor-saving devices offering convenience in this space—microwave ovens, dishwashers, washing machines, dryers, steam cleaning irons, vacuum cleaners, robo cleaners, and now virtual assistants like Amazon's Alexa. The rollout of fifth Generation mobile networks powering the Internet of Things (IoT) even enables your smart refrigerator to order the groceries and have them delivered! Getting your teen to help is thus a stretch, although they could be taught, from a very early age, to make their bed every morning. As Admiral Jim Carrey recounted in his address to the graduating class at the University of Texas, the first task during US Navy SEAL training is making your bed to perfection. Because it not only gives your spirits a lift in having done the first thing in the morning well, but it also teaches that if you do the little things in life better, you can definitely master the bigger things in life too. Besides, it is so relaxing to slip into a well-made bed at the end of a tiring day.

On the positive side, if you are a house-proud parent, it is more likely that your teenager will follow your example. Remember that children's minds are like sponges. From birth, they are watching and constantly absorbing everything their parents do and unconsciously modeling their behavior. Seeing a parent happily engaged in work around the home and sharing the

15

workload is more likely to motivate a teen to join in than daily nagging about tidying up their room. If, on the other hand, they see that you are constantly putting off cleaning and tidying the house, or complaining about cooking, washing up, and cleaning, then they may tend to feel burdened when doing chores themselves.

However, while maintaining a household is a perfect opportunity for teens to learn discipline and grow their self-esteem, modern-day parents are time pressured and stressed. Once upon a time, mothers reigned supreme over the home while fathers went to work as the sole breadwinner. Mothers thus took on the major share of parenting their children as well as maintaining a home sweet home. In educating the girl child the emphasis then was on homemaker skills—cooking, sewing, etiquette, and social graces, as well as being a perfect hostess to support an upwardly mobile husband. This changed as more women pursued education and careers driven by the desire to contribute equally to household income and a better standard of living.

A 2016 study released by the Center for American Progress estimated that 66% of US mothers are either main, sole, or co-earners–highlighting their contribution to household income. This is while they still spend an average of four hours per day doing unpaid domestic work such as cooking, cleaning, and washing which would give them an extra $40,000 annually if it were paid labor according to an Organization for Economic Cooperation and Development (OECD) study. Adding to parental stress is the 12 to 14-hour workday that is the norm for career professionals plus the advent of mobile technology, which keeps employees on call 24-7, 365.

The early teen years are the right age to show your teen that you expect them to contribute to keeping the home well organized and clean. A daily inspection to check if the sheets and duvet are neatly tucked in, the study area is tidied, used clothes are in the laundry basket, the toilet floor is mopped dry, and the water closet is flushed and sanitized is a good practice to instill a hygiene routine. While it is normal for adults to change bed sheets once in two weeks and towels weekly, with pubescent teens, this frequency of change could be shorter. An extra hand towel in the room for a boy to clean up after a nocturnal emission would be useful for maintaining hygiene, too.

Pillowcases in particular need regular changing because the accumulation of dirt and oil plus skin and hair can transfer to the face and block pores. The close contact with other children and sharing of brushes, combs, and headgear during school term or an away game in a sports team could result in the spread of head lice. Often teens may not be aware till the infestation is severe and parents should look out for telltale signs such as an itchy scalp, eggs on the hair shaft, and sores on the scalp, neck, or shoulders. Treatment should begin immediately—some parents use a fine comb on wet hair. Traditional remedies like neem oil or vinegar are not popular with teens because of the odor they leave on the hair. The application of Ivermectin lotion is a very effective and fast way to treat an infection. Irrespective of the method of treatment, all bed linen should be removed, pillows and mattresses aired combs and brushes cleaned and sanitized and floors vacuumed to prevent reinfection.

The golden rule for sanitary napkins is—do not flush them down the toilet. If your goal is to raise an environmentally friendly activist teen, this is a good place to start. The World Economic Forum reported that in the United Kingdom alone between 1.5 to 2 billion sanitary pads and tampons are flushed down the toilet every year. These end up in the sewerage system, are discharged into rivers, and then flow into the sea. Plastic can take between 500-800 years to completely degrade. Meantime they break up into microplastics and fibers and can then enter the food chain. Post menarche, a small bin to hold used pads will help build good disposal habits. Used sanitary napkins should be rolled up and enclosed in the outer cover or wrapped in toilet paper before they are binned. Biodegradable napkins and tampons with nonplastic applicators are on the market and so are compostable ones. These are, of course, more expensive.

Single Tasking Is Smarter Than Multitasking

Too many parents try to manage a busy lifestyle by multi-tasking, but the human brain is not built to support you simultaneously trying to help your child with their homework while crisis managing a work-related emergency on the mobile phone, cooking dinner, and keeping an eye on the evening news. Your brain reacts to this by a process called spotlighting–frantically switching activity between different areas of the brain as your focus changes, leaving you mentally and emotionally drained by the day's end. Multitasking reduces attention spans and makes it more difficult to concentrate while it reduces your ability to read the emotional reactions playing out in each situation (Professor Clifford Nass, Stanford TEDx talk). Single-tasking allows you to be in the moment and give your undivided attention to interacting with your teen, work colleague, partner, friend, or the task at hand. You might remember your parents saying, "Listen to me while I talk to you!" during your teenage years but are now finding it impossible to get your own teen to do this because you now have to compete with a screen as well as the teenager's natural inclination to rebel.

By making single-tasking a habit, you can feel more energized by giving yourself time to recharge physical and mental energy used up and avoid feeling drained out and irritable. Maintaining a to-do list helps you plan this effectively and sets an example for your teen to follow. Research shows that the brain is at work retrieving and organizing everything that happened during the day while we sleep and making us more prepared and recharged for the next morning. Organizing your schedule, considering the obstacles, and thinking of ways to overcome them could help you wake up to a "eureka" moment the next morning. Traditional wisdom called this "sleeping things over." Another benefit of making a habit of planning together is that your family knows your commitments outside of the home and could be more considerate by not interrupting your work.

Most of us are either early birds or night owls and scheduling more complex or intensive work when we are at our best gives better results and less grief. Be careful not to impose your preference on others, though. Each one is different and some degree of compromise to accommodate individual preferences will contribute to family harmony.

Family Meetings Teach Democracy in the Home

A good way to build family harmony and set an example of democracy in action is to set up a regular "family time" where every member of the family can bring up or talk about any topic that interests or concerns them. This can be carved out from the weekly routine—for example, Friday dinner or Sunday Lunch. Apart from allowing the family to spend uninterrupted time together, this allows your teen to participate in democracy in action (in the home) and is actually early experience in managing interpersonal politics, which can lead to greater self-confidence and self-esteem as an adult. After all, democracy is about diverse viewpoints, inclusivity, compromise, negotiation, consensus, and cooperation. And family activities like movies, games, holidays, and travel can be opportunities for teens to develop these essential skills. Some time could be spent on discussing current affairs and citizen activism in shaping the world. These may not be topics covered in the formal education system but with the potential to significantly impact their future. As a millennial, the World Wide Web was science fiction reading in your teen years, but you have had to rapidly adapt to how it has changed the way you live, work, and play. The only confident prediction we can make about the future world is that it will be significantly different from the present.

Many families have pets for the simple reason that they are great companions and fun for their teens. Some teens may even find it easier to hug a pet rather than a member of the family! And pets are a good way to encourage your teen to be more involved with household chores through feeding, grooming, cleaning up, and generally taking responsibility for their well-being. Visits to the Veterinary Clinic, caring for a sick pet, and overcoming grief over the death of a pet, lead to discussions about life, death, and emotions that lay the foundation for the future teen's mental health.

Chapter 3:

Be Organized

Don't be afraid to change. You may lose something good but you may gain something better. –Anon

In the larger scheme of things, being organized requires your teen to balance four interconnected, yet distinct, aspects of life—studies, sports, social life, and society. All of these are equally important to be a balanced and confident adult and require the soft skills that are addressed in later chapters. This chapter deals with the more functional aspects that support and encourage a teen to be self-disciplined, organized, and self-reliant.

Studies are top of mind because every parent knows that education provides stability in life and opens doors for their children. Apart from examinations being a formal test of knowledge and ability, employers consider them an indication of grit and perseverance, which they assume to be an indicator of the potential to master skills and develop in a career. Keep track of your teen's academic calendar to avoid scheduling family activity that clashes with their examination timetables—midterms, term end, and year-end. The average teen, no matter how well prepared, finds exams stressful. Clearing your own schedules during this time and for at least two weeks prior helps in bringing reassurance and a sense of support, even if you are not actively supervising their preparation. You might have been their home tutor during the toddler and tween years, and this would give you a sense of their academic ability as well as study style. Some children like to read their textbooks out loud. Others will make summaries of their content to use as revision notes before an exam. Some will try the exercises in the textbook or look for past questions and answers. Others might turn to texting their best friend to decide on which sections to study.

Online tutoring is now a big business and growing even faster after classroom learning was restricted during the pandemic. Sal Khan, the founder of the Khan Academy, was one of the first to offer free online supplemental material through short video tutorials starting with physics but now in almost every subject. There are many sites that provide fee-based one-on-one sessions, too, with personalized work plans or group sessions.

Developing an interest in a subject is a great motivation for learning as well as academic and career success. Some parents push their children to be in the top one percent in their grade and expect top performance in every subject. But academic success is not a reliable predictor of career success since it does not measure leadership, the ability to take risks, or networking skills—all requisites for innovation, entrepreneurship, and success at the higher echelons of management. Of course, good grades do indicate grit and self-discipline and a high GPA score does give your children an advantage in job applications, especially in a recessionary economy. As the world shifts to a knowledge-based economy, talent and deep specialized knowledge can help in breaking the mold–Steve Jobs and Bill Gates were not known for academic brilliance and probably did not even turn in their homework assignments in time.

Sports are a wonderful way to prepare teens for meeting the challenges of life. Education and sports complement each other like yin and yang—a perfect balance of mind and body. Sports build character by teaching your teen to accept victory and defeat with the same equanimity, just as it instills resilience, responsibility, and teamwork and builds individual pride in mastery of skills. Overprotective parents tend to worry about sports-related injuries hampering their teens' development, but all sports are not physical. Chess and scrabble are examples of noncontact sports. Video games and the increasingly popular e-gaming also teach problem-solving, sharpen reflexes, and stimulate the mind but this tends to be a solitary activity and could deprive your teen of the interaction and camaraderie that creates lifelong friendships and affiliation which is another positive benefit of team games. Online sports can be very competitive too, and lead to bullying and harassment with severe mental health implications for an immature teen unless addressed in time.

Guide Your Teen to "Living Outside"

Aside from sports, you could help your teen develop greater confidence through adventure-based activities offered by theme parks, water parks, and nature trails. Water sports are good for overcoming the fear of heights, the fear of water, and the fear of falling. If as a millennial you are not a fan of roller coasters, you might find the idea of accompanying your teen on their first ride terrifying, but be brave and you too will soon overcome your fear. Learning to swim and ride a bicycle at an early age not only helps maintain fitness but adds to your child's freedom, self-confidence, and self-esteem.

Encouraging your teen to participate in an active social life may help them build lifelong friendships. If you reflect back on your own childhood, next to your family, your bonds with childhood friends are still the strongest because you have known them for longer. And, even after many years, those bonds are rekindled very quickly. Children love celebrating birthdays but a word of caution for younger teens if you are not able to accommodate the entire class it may cause those classmates left out to feel slighted. The way out could be to treat the class at school. Always though, make it a rule that your teen attends every party they are invited to, and you speak to the parents to thank them. This opportunity to network informally with other parents can be invaluable in crisis situations. If at all possible, maintain an open house policy for your teen's friends.

Community service, volunteering, special interest clubs, performing arts, music, visual arts, and debating are other options besides sports to learn teamwork and problem-solving skills, gain self-esteem, create closer friendships outside the classroom, and open their mind to a diversity of views. They also enable your teen to explore their natural talent and enhance their college applications and paid scholarship prospects.

Good Habits Last a Lifetime

Private boarding schools that are uniquely British institutions still found in the United Kingdom and the British Commonwealth have a long tradition of excellence in producing high achievers, but the disadvantage is that your teen, although they may be well looked after, will miss the love that only parents and close family can give them. Of course, private boarding schools are expensive and not everyone can afford them. Besides, they are not popular in the US, which has only about 35,000 students attending them out of a total of 48.1 million according to data from the National Center for Education Statistics.

So, it is really up to the majority of parents to instill organization and discipline in children. This can start with demarcating spaces in the house for your teen. A teen's bedroom, of course, should be a cozy sleeping space, a study, and a hang-out area for friends with a closet or wardrobe, dresser, chair, and good lighting. Television is not recommended, but today a mobile phone, tablet, or laptop gives access to streaming entertainment platforms like Netflix and Disney and gaming, which is now reported to be averaging around 69 minutes per day.

Bedrooms are not ideal study spaces because they are associated with sleep and relaxation. A dedicated study space is better for concentrating and retaining information.

Making your child responsible for cleaning, decluttering, and maintaining these spaces is excellent for instilling basic discipline. A planner or calendar serves to keep track of upcoming events and helps parents plan their routines while accommodating their teens while maintaining a journal or a to-do list reinforces your teen's sense of accomplishment and could train them to single tasks rather than being reactive and multitasking. There is now an app for everything, and schedule planning is not an exception—Trello, Evernote, Busy Kid, or even the plain, vanilla-flavored Google calendar will help your teen be organized and in control of their time.

Chapter 4:

Inner Beauty

Outer beauty attracts, but inner beauty captivates. –Kate Angell, author, "Squeeze Play."

Although trained in personal hygiene from the toddler years onwards, your young teen is now independent and no longer under parental supervision when brushing their teeth, bathing, or getting dressed. You assume that they will follow the routine you have taught them, but a sniff test and occasional gentle reminders may be necessary. In personal hygiene too, it is important to remember that parents are role models. This may also be a good time to explain the science behind the routines even though as a toddler a visit to the dentist could help in checking on jaw size, teeth crowding, and even mouth breathing, which could affect the correct development of the palette.

Early teens are the age when the secondary molars develop. For a generation that virtually cut their teeth on visual mediums like TikTok and YouTube videos, perfect teeth are essential for the perfect smile. An all-clear from the dentist on these issues is a relief but proper oral hygiene is still needed to avoid tooth decay and gingivitis. But you could explain to your teen that as scientific research progresses, it finds more evidence linking good health to personal hygiene. For example, good dental hygiene prevents plaque buildup on teeth, which can lead to heart disease or regular hand washing can help prevent bacteria on your hands from infecting the pimples on your face. In the early stages of the COVID-19 pandemic, everyone was reminded to wash their hands frequently and cover their mouths when coughing or sneezing. But as time passed and fatigue set in, these good hygiene practices were increasingly forgotten.

The twice-daily routine of brushing teeth can be supplemented with flossing, and oral thrush or bad breath tackled with an antiseptic mouthwash. It is known that the left hemisphere of the brain is associated with logic and language skills and controls the right hand, while the right hemisphere, associated with creativity and intuition, controls the left hand. This has led to the myth that the 10% of the population that is left-handed is smarter. This is not necessarily true, but whichever is your dominant hand, you can have some fun and wake up both hemispheres of the brain by using both hands alternatively to brush your teeth. Conventional wisdom says brushing for two minutes is essential, so try one minute with each hand. It may be difficult at first but as you improve with practice you also start each day with a small sense of achievement to boost your confidence as you become increasingly more comfortable in using your non-dominant hand.

A suitable skin cleansing routine based on skin type and the use of gentle cleansers and moisturizers will definitely help your teen's confidence because glowing skin instantly communicates good health and well-being.

Is social media amplifying light-skin bias? Colorism, the within-group and between-groups prejudice that favors light skin, is a global cultural norm that appears to have been intensified by Instagram and TikTok, and its promise is amplified by skin whitening creams. It can lead to comments from classmates such as, "Oh, you are too black, you are ugly," which can have a devastating effect on the teen's mind. Parents may struggle to explain colorism, which has its roots in colonialism and the slave trade when there were subtle practices to divide Black people like only allowing lighter-skinned people to work inside a house. This created an intraracial prejudice, but it is only one such issue amongst others such as sexism, fatphobia, featurism, and queerphobia. Apart from social media influences, colorism can show up in real-world experiences, such as preferential treatment shown to those with lighter skin tones. To manage the toxic damage that can be inflicted on young minds, parents should seek out support groups online and add their voices to countering trends that are exploiting colorism and similar biases for profit. One example that may resonate with your teen is the computer-generated fictional avatar, the rapper FN Meka who collected millions of followers and views on TikTok. Capitol Records Music Group signing up the AI-generated FN Meka in early 2022 caused a huge backlash against a black culture stereotype being signed up by a major record label when there was plentiful exceptional real-life talent available. The huge negative reaction on social media was successful in pressuring Capitol Records to drop the deal within 24 hours.

The Onset of Puberty Signals Major Challenges Ahead

With the average age of puberty dropping to the pre-teen years, you need to be alert to signs that your child may be struggling to cope and in need of support. This could particularly affect the girl child if she comes of age before her classmates and can manifest itself as a sleep disorder, mood swings, or anxiety attacks. Some cultures celebrate coming of age with ceremonies to signify the increased responsibilities that mark this milestone. But in the US, Canada, and Europe "Sweet 16," the 16th birthday is more likely to be celebrated with a formal reception for family and friends than the actual milestone of menarche.

Puberty is not only a time of physical changes but changes to body shape make children feel awkward as their head, face and hands may grow faster than the upper body and limbs, and boys' voices will crack as the larynx grows and facial and body hair starts to grow. This is a time of brain development too with "brain pruning" which is the reduction of excess gray matter or cortical thinning which researchers have linked through brain imaging and personality tests to greater maturity, conscientiousness, and emotional stability. This is also the time when planning, decision-making, and problem-solving skills develop and parents should support this growing maturity by acknowledging their teens' opinions, gradually giving them more responsibility and freedom. Paradoxically, this is the time that the outside world and their peers influence teens' behavior while family stability greatly influences their personality development. Stress brought on by the loss of a parent or a divorce during this time increases neuroticism, which can persist in the adult too, according to a 2017 US study quoted by BBC Future.

On the practical side, keeping track of menstrual patterns and being prepared can help avoid embarrassment for girls in school and there are now period panties that can absorb and hold menstrual flow. However, the more commonly used products, such as tampons and pads, need to be changed regularly based on the volume of flow. Girls would normally lose an average of between 60–80 ml over the four to five days of their period, with the initial flow being around 20 ml. Your teen may not want to try menstrual cups if the sight of blood makes them feel squeamish, although they are safe, reusable, eco-friendly, and save users from having to find disposal bins as is the case with pads and tampons. It could take a few tries before finding the right fit, shape, and size to hold the menstrual flow without overflowing or leaking and mastering the art of inserting the cup, but menstrual cups are gaining popularity because of comfort and being free to swim or maintain a sports or fitness routine if your energy levels permit.

Puberty Is a Challenging Time for Self-Image

For boys, this can be an awkward age too as they lose puppy fat and become physically stronger. Both boys and girls are prone to acne due to hormonal changes, making their skins more oily, resulting in the sebaceous glands being prone to bacterial infection that causes acne. Acne makes teens more self-conscious, and it affects 85-90% of teens, up to 30% could have severe acne with boys more prone to it than girls.

Along with puberty comes the growth of body hair. Softer vellum hair also known as "peachy fuzz" that grows on most of the body is generally OK but the thicker terminal hair that grows on the upper lip as a mustache, beard growth, underarm, and pubic hair can be problematic as they grow thicker and more prominent as puberty progresses. In the case of boys, shaving is a sign of manliness, but girls may prefer to use longer-lasting methods even though lady shaver models, which are gentler on the skin than traditional razors, are available in both electric and rechargeable options.

While contemporary beauty is promoted as a smooth, glowing hairless body, it does have its roots (pun intended) in the fact that perspiration is essential to cool the body (especially due to exercise, exertion, or outside temperature). The sweat glands in the armpit and groin produce a thicker, milky fluid. Sweat by itself has no smell, but the thicker hair in these parts traps sweat, allowing odor-causing bacteria to grow. The problem with shaving these areas is that it is temporary and hair regrows within a few days. And while this happens, it can be uncomfortable and prickly. Tweezing is painful. Depilatory creams and lotions after a shower or wax strips offer longer-lasting effects—generally about a month but should be used with caution and tested for allergy. Hot wax treatment and laser removal offer longer-lasting effects because they remove or damage the hair follicles but need to be performed under expert care. Deodorizers and antiperspirants are a solution too, but underarm hair embarrasses girls due to fashion trends such as skinny tops, sleeveless dresses, and also if they are swimmers, water sports enthusiasts, or sportswomen.

Chapter 5:

First Impressions Count

Style is a way to say who you are without having to speak. –Rachel Zoe, fashion designer.

Media, music, movies, television, sports, and the Internet play a role, but the most significant influence on teens' fashion choices is their peers. Teens are eager to fit in and use fashion to maintain their friendships and boost their self-esteem. Fearful of rejection and humiliation, they ask friends for fashion advice, and their sense of style and brands are influenced by celebrities, fashion magazines, designer brands, and social media influencers. Teens dress to draw attention and girls in particular can be obsessed with body image, which even leads them to follow unhealthy food habits in an effort to be like their favorite idol. Since young teens are growing fast, clothes do not last long, and anyway, no girl, or woman for that matter, will wear the same dress twice to formal events. The young teen wardrobe is heavy on casual wear and light on formal clothes. Shoes and accessories are essentials, too. Girls feel underdressed unless their accessories and shoes match their outfit. Early teens will begin to experiment with makeup and fragrances too, but mainly at home or on playdates with friends.

The Way You Dress Expresses Your Personality

This is a time of experimentation because fashion is an expression of their personality, which is still developing as they progress and mature during their teen years. Of course, you need to be conscious that as a parent your fashion style is an influence on them too. As a mother, if you habitually dress in punk or grunge rock or flamboyant style, you cannot expect your teen to accept being dressed in traditional style, and anyway, your friends and peers will find this funny too. If you live in a community that is very conservative, culturally and socially, a modest dress style will be the default option for your family. If not, most families dress mostly in modern urban style and you might consider any of the following as an appropriate starter for girls—the girly look, preppy, geeky and nerdy style, casual or casual chic. Boys will similarly be influenced by their fathers to adopt a casual or classical dress style. Nerdy, geeky, is a unisex style.

The power of a good hairstyle should not be underestimated. Even a simple dress with a good hairstyle that complements the shape of your face and features can make you unforgettable. It also signals that you take good care of yourself because good hair care is essential to making hair manageable and good looking. Pulling hair is a teenage coping tool for stress but excessive pulling resulting in bald patches can be a sign of mental illness and require professional help. Being increasingly self-conscious due to puberty, falling hair can be worrying for teens and they could ask you for an explanation. Hormonal changes will trigger some hair fall. It is a natural mechanism to replace damaged scalp and hair. Nutrition, heredity, and menstrual complications can be reasons for increased hair fall.

Medications such as for acne could temporarily increase hair fall too.

The Circular Fashion Revolution

Fashion and dress styles can be a good launch pad for family discussions around the issues that can shape your teen's personality. For example, the environmental cost of the fashion industry—it takes 10,000 liters of water to make a pair of jeans. Similarly, making a pair of sneakers typically generates 13.6 kg of Carbon Dioxide, and global production accounts for 1.4% of global greenhouse gas emissions, compared to 2.5% for air travel according to makefashionbetter.com. A good reason to shop secondhand (pre-owned retail is the new name for this growing trend), looking for eco-friendly brands or donating clothes that are no longer used. Supporting the circular fashion industry is a good cause.

Flamboyant colors can be attention-getting but also jarring to the eyes. A color wheel is a useful tool for discussions on contrasting and complementary shades of color. You might already have initiated an early discussion of the color palette when redecorating or renovating your home or even when admiring the colors that nature presents in a beautiful sunrise or sunset, a pristine seashore, or a crystal clear stream on a family holiday. Being influenced by nature is a counter to artful and insincere influences on social media that strive to sell by playing on teen insecurities.

Washing clothes and ironing are essential to appear well-groomed. Showing your teen how to operate a washing machine and how to safely handle a hot iron and the settings for different fabrics is a must. One way to get teens to do their own laundry is to designate one day of the week for each member of the family to do their own washing. Modern washing machines have a cupboard dry function and clothes can be folded and put away directly from the machine—useful in maintaining bedrooms neat and uncluttered.

Chapter 6:

Healthy Bodies, Healthy Minds

It is not selfish to love yourself, take care of yourself, make your happiness a priority. It's necessary. –Mandy Hale, New York Times bestselling author

Early teens need parental help and oversight in taking care of their health. They are not mature enough to seek care on their own or self-medicate or be trusted to take the correct dosages of prescription medicines. They are also too young to apply for health insurance and will be covered through family insurance cover. Even for busy parents, a health emergency is a time for tender loving care and attention. However, children are susceptible to catching infections at school, and with their brains and bodies experiencing a growth spurt, early teens can be sometimes uncoordinated and prone to minor accidents. A good enough reason to teach them essential hygiene, basic first aid, and how to get help in emergencies.

Always Be Connected to Basics

Since babies are literally born these days with a cell phone in their hands, program an emergency contact number on their phone. This is easier to access directly on an iPhone but can be done on the contact list in an Android phone. Voice activation through Apple Siri, Google voice, or Amazon Alexa can be useful for them to know about too. GPS tracking apps allow you to track your child's location in addition to parental control and monitoring phone use. You may have already warned them about sharing phone numbers with strangers, clicking on unknown links, and sending photos of themselves.

Home medicine cabinets are usually placed beyond the reach of young children, so having a backup pack of basic supplies such as band-aids, cotton wool, an antiseptic cream, or lotion in an accessible drawer or closet may be a good idea. Most medical professionals now say ice is the first-line treatment for cuts, bumps, sprains, and bruises. Having an ice pack, ice cubes or a small plastic bottle of chilled water in your refrigerator is useful in emergencies. Again, if the freezer is too high or too deep for a teen to reach, an ice-cold bottle should always be easily accessible on a lower shelf. Train your child to seek help as soon as possible from a responsible adult if sick, injured or otherwise distressed. Teens sometimes tend to hide health issues due to fear of blame, but this should not be a problem if you maintain open communication and trust.

Hygiene First and Be Ready for Emergencies

If your child is asthmatic, their puffer or allergy spray should be carried at all times along with a note on possible triggers to avoid. Food allergies are common too and despite best intentions, could be triggered unknowingly either in school or out of school. Since it may be difficult for a distressed child to communicate clearly, it is best to be prepared by sharing information on the allergens with the school or a responsible person in the out-of-school activity or group.

A useful skill to teach children early is to identify contaminated food which can cause nausea, vomiting, diarrhea, and in extreme cases lead to food poisoning. They can also contract and suffer from stomach bugs by touching surfaces that could be contaminated and the best way to avoid this is by washing hands frequently with soap and water, especially before eating.

Carrying a small pack of hand sanitizer, made popular during the Covid pandemic, is also a good practice.

Children can start swimming lessons either with a coach or under family supervision when they are tall enough to stand with their noses above the waterline in the baby or junior pool. This is generally when a toddler is between three to four years. Starting as early as possible is best because relaxing your body and coordinated kicking is the basic skill of floating and moving forward, which then allows you to learn the strokes to propel yourself. Overcoming the fear of water is another step that builds self-confidence.

By the early teen years, it is possible that your teen has already learned to ride a bicycle. If not, it is a good time to start. Even if they had learned to ride when younger, rides would be mostly under parental supervision or riding together as a family. In their teen years, they are ready to enjoy the freedom of riding independently, which allows them to meet up with neighborhood friends or run small errands. Of course, if starting to learn they must also be taught road rules and safe riding before being given total freedom.

Chapter 7:

The Cycle of Life

"In the midst of life, we are in death," wrote Martin Luther in 1527. This makes it easier to explain death to your child if you are open and approachable in your conversations with them, starting from the opportunities that will arise from the inquisitive toddler years onwards. For example, the BBC has released a viewership figure of 52% of the UK population aged 4+ watched at least 3 minutes of the funeral ceremonies for Queen Elizabeth II. The global viewership figures are not known, although there are unverified claims of 4.1 billion. Obviously, this intense coverage would have sparked questions in many young children's minds. Many parents did actually bring young children with them when they lined the funeral route, too.

Apart from high-profile events like this, a death in the extended family, friends, or neighbors, and news of accidents and tragedies would trigger their curiosity. A family album or a book that you are reading together may have triggered their curiosity, too. Hopefully, you would be open and honest in explaining death and be mindful of speaking to their age. What is most important is to help children manage their emotions of loss and sadness, be understanding and supportive, avoid causing fear and distress, and arrange activities that will help them to recover. Losing a parent, grandparent or a well-loved relative will be more stressful and lead them to grieve for a longer time. The loss of a pet can be very distressing too, although the experience of caring for a pet who is sick and needs to be put down is an opportunity for children to learn to manage grief. At such times, parents need to support their teens to manage their emotions while overcoming their own grief and sense of loss. You will always be their role model.

Religion provided the structure to keep society running smoothly for previous generations. The role of organized religion though has been declining and currently, 35% of millennials say they have no religious affiliation (2014). What is surprising though is that there is no corresponding decline in spirituality and 72% of millennials say they are spiritual. Belief in God and prayer remain at the same level as Gen X. To quote Astrophysicist Neil DeGrasse Tyson, "the universe is within us."

The Destiny of the Soul Is the Common Thread

With the rise of science and the explosion of scientific knowledge questioning basic tenets of religion such as creation, hitherto monolithic structures have fragmented into religious sects. This has led to the rise of fundamentalism across the world with Born Again churches and religious sectarianism. In some countries, including the USA, a more virulent form is seen to be emerging as religious nationalism. In some countries, this has led to entrenched authoritarian governance although in the USA it is still a rising tide of white nationalism that competes in the democratic space.

Paul Robertson in a TEDx talk offered a contemporary definition for religion as "... a set of beliefs and practices relevant to non-obvious beings." This is broad enough to encompass all the major faiths. Humanity is now conditioned to think that anything that cannot be scientifically proven does not exist. The telescope and the microscope have replaced faith and belief. But the question of "who created what" is still unanswered. Even as researchers launch even more powerful telescopes like the James Webb to peer billions of light years into the origins of the Universe, what came before the big bang that launched their journey through the cosmos is still a mystery. Similarly, science has established that conception happens when an ovum is fertilized by a sperm but the question of when a human person begins is still not clear. The controversial repeal of Roe v. Wade in the US and the patchwork of pro-life state legislation ranging from outright banning at conception to within 6 to 26 weeks proves this point.

Most of the questions about death are about what happens after. A surprising fact is that although organized religion seems out of fashion and a major cause of worldwide strife, at its core, all five major religions are united by the concept of the soul or "life spirit." Christianity is based on Plato's philosophy of a mortal body and an immortal soul while Judaism and Islam believe that the soul is breathed in by God at conception. The three faiths believe death separates body and soul, which then remains in limbo in a state of spiritual consciousness awaiting redemption or damnation depending on the virtue and morality displayed in life. Hinduism and Buddhism are both based on the idea of reincarnation of the soul—it is destined to live forever in an eternal cycle of death and rebirth. However, Buddhists aim to break free of this cycle by an accumulation of merit, which is based on your own actions in this life through mindful living and charity, and also transferred to you through "dana" or almsgiving remembrances after you are gone.

Movies like Disney and Pixar's *Soul* present the idea of the afterlife in a contemporary setting and may be helpful in starting a discussion with your teen.

Teens and Sex—Drawing the Line Between Normative and Problematic Behavior

Your 10-year-old will know more about sexual behavior today than the average 20-year-old did when entering university. This is not only because they have more access to information on the internet and through mainstream media coverage of sexual orientation. Their millennial parents are reported to be having fewer sexual partners than their parents did (8 down from 12) but are more accepting of pre-marital sex and homosexuality, which normalizes discussion of these topics in the family. Jean M. Twenge Ph.D. the author of "Generation Me" and Professor of Psychology at San Diego State attributes the shift to growing "cultural individualism"—noting that amongst other things, song lyrics are now written as "I," "Me," and "You" rather than plural pronouns "We" and "Us." She says, "When culture places more needs on the self and less on social rules, more relaxed attitudes towards sexuality are the inevitable result." Thus, even if you are unsure of the right time to talk to your teen and the amount of information they need, be assured that they may confide in you the latest gossip brought from home to school by their best friends and schoolmates.

Spending time with your teen and keeping the door open for such conversations on sexual behavior at unexpected times like in the car, watching TV, or on holiday is the best approach to addressing your teen's need to have accurate information. The more trust your teen has in you plus a supportive yet non intrusive family environment helps them get information to safely navigate the increased curiosity in their bodies, feelings of attraction, and the desire to experiment that occurs with the progress of puberty. By the time they are ten, the majority of children would also have had some level of sexual education communicated through schools, media, and peers. A minority may even have experimented with sex play or been subject to explorative sexual behavior. More normally, with the onset of puberty, self-touch and masturbatory behavior will be common and boys will likely have wet dreams, which is why it is good to educate them about nocturnal emission early, similar to educating girls about menstruation because it eases them from being embarrassed when it happens.

Because teens are not as mature as adults, they are more likely to be impulsive, take risks, and be less concerned about the future consequences of their actions. As a parent, you may have taught them to respect limits by explaining right and wrong, what is acceptable and what is not through play activity in their toddler and pre-teen years, and this is a time to further reinforce those early lessons. Teach your teen how to say "no" while being friendly but firm. Risky behavior in teens is most often related to alcohol, drugs, or sex. Since early teen sexual behavior is driven by experimentation (with either the same sex or the opposite sex), this may be a good time to pre-emptively reinforce the need for consent and that your teen understands that even though permission may be given, it can also be withdrawn later and this needs to be respected gracefully. By having a respectful family environment in which important decisions are made through discussion and consensus, your teen could already be well-schooled in this skill. Since sexual attitudes start young your teen needs to be aware too of sexually transmitted diseases, safe sex through the use of condoms and dental dams, pregnancy, and domestic abuse. Talk also to your teens about early sexual behavior to reassure them that it is not a permanent indication of sexual attitudes, which can change in later life.

The latest estimates from the US Centers for Disease Control and Prevention show that one in every five US citizens would be suffering from Sexually Transmitted Infections (STIs) on any given day (CDC, 2018). Probable causes and symptoms of STIs need to be part of the conversations you have with your teen. Going through a long list of the 20 STIs plus HIV/AIDS and the more recent Monkeypox is not practical though, especially due to the notoriously short attention span of a teen. What seems more practical is to talk about the symptoms that commonly indicate a possible infection. This should suffice since further treatment requires consulting a medical practitioner or vising a sexual health clinic. The common symptoms in a girl are itching around the vagina or discharge, unusual bleeding from the vagina, sores, blisters, or bumps around the vagina, anus, or mouth, and unusual pain when peeing or during bowel movement. Boys should look out for pain when peeing, burning or itching in the penis, discharge or drip from the penis, sores, bumps, or blisters around the genitals, anus, or mouth.

Make your teen aware that unprotected sex is not the sole cause of STIs, and that proper hygiene helps prevent infections, as well. Sharing a razor, sheets, towels, or clothes, kissing, and sharing contaminated food, are also possible spreaders of STIs. They can spread through blood transfusions too, but recent advances in screening potential blood donors have all but eliminated this possibility.

Keeping screen time to a minimum and increasing family interaction time may be necessary because this is a period when teens may withdraw into their own world and be less communicative. You may really have to work hard to get them to share what is happening in their lives and, importantly, listen carefully to understand without being intrusive. Teens are entitled to their private time too.

Neglected Teens Are Soft Targets for Gangs

You can watch out for early signs of troubling issues by lightly monitoring the peer group your teen is hanging out with. Have they moved away from previously close friends? What is causing them to do this? What is happening in their sports, society, and social circles? Having these conversations as part of a regular routine helps your teen to unburden their worries and stresses and also lets them know they can depend on you as a confidant. When parents do not play this role teens are more likely to drift away and seek support from their peer group which can then make them more vulnerable to risky behavior because of pressure to fit in. These conversations with your teen are also important to counter the impact and influence of media stereotypes, violence in movies, and misinformation–whether shared by peers or online and help your teen in maintaining emotional balance and adjusting to the physical changes of puberty. When and how to deliver information on romance, intimacy, sexual orientation, and sexual behavior, practicing safe sex will always be a delicate balance between listening to your teen and being open to when they want to have such conversations. Forcing the issue based on your own timing can be counterproductive.

Encourage Curiosity About Pregnancy and Childbirth

If your teen does not have a younger sibling, this may be the time when they want to know more about "Where do babies come from?" Sometimes, this may be triggered by visiting a friend or relative to greet a newborn, seeing a pregnant lady on the street, in a movie, or even reading a story. You may have already passed the sperm meets an egg stage of explanation and can let them know as they grew older that pregnancy happens through penis in vagina sexual intercourse. If you have not shared this information by adolescence, there is every possibility that your teen would seek it from their friends, media, or at school, and you would not have control over that information or misinformation that is shared. It is easier to be the source of information than to fact-check and correct misinformation.

Sex education is not one big lecture that you can deliver and be done with. Instead, it is a series of small conversations which start in the toddler years with the correct identification of body parts and are repeated and expanded on as they grow. Teens who have had good sex education prior to puberty have less risky sexual behavior and more stable relationships as adults.

Your teen will now be in grade seven and learning biology. Homework too can be the base on which you explain the stages of pregnancy and childbirth. Again, not in one big lecture but in small conversations based on your teen's attention span. This would be a good time to check your teen's knowledge of safe sex and contraception and talk to them about it.

Even if your teen does not have access to pornography due to parental controls on their smart devices, they could be exposed to it through their peers or referred to in sex education class. Thus, you should be prepared for questions about anal and oral penetrative sex, intercrural "thigh" sex, mutual masturbation, scissoring or tribbing (girl on girl or girl on boy), and group sex. Hark back to your own childhood and flicking through your parents' magazines or VHS tapes and DVDs. Remind them that porn is fiction or fantasy, which is why most people watch it, and the reality may be different and not as enjoyable as what is portrayed on screen.

You may also want to have a discussion around the fact that the porn industry, similar to the beauty and fashion industries, objectifies people, particularly women. Being comfortable in their own body and not trying to fit into an ideal male or female as portrayed by the media and advertisers is essential for self-confidence and self-esteem. Be confident and friendly when your teen wants answers, but listen carefully first so that you engage with them with the right amount of information and make your teen feel that you are open to helping them process and make sense of sensitive topics.

Chapter 8:

Words Matter

Listening......ignites the human mind. –Nancy Kline, Author of "Time to Think"

You might think it odd to start a chapter on helping teens to communicate better with a quote on listening. If you are like many parents, "listen to me when I talk to you!" is probably the most frequently used phrase in conversations with your teen. This unfortunately is likely to trigger typical teenage behavior of either finding fault with you as a parent or behaving childishly by slamming doors and crying. Not a good example of effective communication for your teens. An oft-repeated truism is that people remember how you made them feel long after they have forgotten what you did for them. If the opinion polls are accurate, it seems that the American voter is poised to deliver this message to the incumbent administration in the upcoming midterm elections.

Nancy Kline reminisces that the greatest gift their mother gave to her and her two siblings was that she listened to them and gave them time and space to think. Creating a listening environment in the family is the greatest gift a parent can give their children because they will carry that with them to their adult relationships.

Communication need not always be about problems and schoolwork. Sharing a joke, being funny, mentioning a bright spot in your workday, evening commute or an experience of a friend or colleague helps open up communication in the family. If your teen has a different point of view, appreciate their

49

perspective, even though they may not be mature enough to fully appreciate the situation. Most importantly, show them that you care.

Listen With Your Eyes and Ears to See Clearly

Author and entrepreneur Christine Comaford, in a widely viewed TED Talks, claims the average person has 60,000 thoughts per day and 90% of them are repetitive. Added to this is the modern distraction of the mobile phone, and the "always on" news cycle. Think how many times you are in a conversation and suddenly you realize that you have absolutely no idea what has just been said. This is because your mind has wandered off to think about your next meeting, a phone call you need to return, something happening in the background, or what to make for dinner. One technique to overcome this and be in the present moment is based on the Japanese concept of "ma" meaning space. It suggests you focus on the blank space between two thoughts, gradually expanding this space. Imagine your thoughts are like a newsfeed at the bottom of a TV screen and focus on the space between them, letting your thoughts pass without holding on or clinging to them. Gradually you will notice the empty space between thoughts increasing. Practice this technique for 5 minutes over the next 30 days and you will see a significant change in your ability to concentrate on the person or task in front of you.

By training yourself to pay attention and listen, you are able to meaningfully engage with your child beginning from the toddler and pre-teen years when children are attention seekers—incurably curious about the world around them, and at the same time their brains are like sponges absorbing your every word and action. These experiences anchor their future adult personality, and you will help them become better communicators because they too learn the habit of actively listening to understand emotions rather than reacting to words. If you have not created this bond early, you may find it difficult to communicate with your teen because they are now more withdrawn due to the changes occurring with puberty, wanting more independence and anxious about peer acceptance, thus open to outside influence. But do not give up hope. Now you need to work harder, spend more time with your teen, making them feel connected to family. Research shows that teens with stronger family bonds are less likely to engage in risky behavior.

You communicate not only verbally but also through your body language. The problem with this is that we live behind our faces. This means you do not see that your facial expression when responding to your teen may be at odds with your words. Sometimes you may think your words are meant to be encouraging, but your face shows fear or worry. Research says our emotions work 400 times faster than our intellect. This is specifically true of teens because evolution is priming the way the brain works, to keep them safe in the outside world, through quicker emotional responses that trigger flight or fight. Your facial expression is based on emotions that have in turn been shaped by the care and attention you received as a child from your family as they coped with the realities of home life when you were growing up. As you strive to give your teen a better future, you may need to pay attention to breaking the mold that made you too. When you accept and reveal your real self and pay attention to actively listen, you are creating a caring and nurturing environment in the home and role-modeling behavior that makes your teen an empathetic adult who will do better socially and academically.

Comaford herself says that when she was seven, her father told her that she should have been a boy because she was neither pretty nor smart as a girl. She says this immediately led her to constantly question "Am I good enough?" and drove her to be constantly exhausted by trying to prove her father wrong through overachieving in her professional and business career while she explored her personal quest for meaning. Be careful what you wish for your children.

Help Your Teen Own the Solution

Your brain is hardwired by society into thinking that if your teen or anyone else comes to you with a problem, it means that they are incapable of finding the solution. Very often, you jump in with advice or a solution while they are halfway through explaining their problem. When your teen argues or seems unconvinced, you continue to offer alternatives or changes until they agree or go away. Now you think the problem is solved, but after some time it resurfaces. Your solution was not wrong. In fact, it may be perfect, logical, and exactly what the other person may have done anyway too. But it does not get implemented because you own it, not them. The next time, try giving them all your attention, rephrasing what they said to show that you understand, asking clarifying questions if necessary, and remaining in companionable silence while their mind processes options and arrives at the solution. After all, the brain that created the problem is perfectly capable of coming up with the solution too!

Remember that life does not arrive with a roadmap and every person is unique. Best seek professional help though if school performance drops along with frequent outbursts of anger and rebellion against authority, changes of mood, or signs of depression.

Keyboards, Pens, Texting, and Cyber Slang

With the introduction of Common Core State Standards in 2010, US schools removed cursive writing from the curriculum since proficiency in handwriting was no longer required. Finland followed in 2016 and even in the United Kingdom fully cursive writing is no longer on the national curriculum. However, the debate of whether the pen is still mightier than the keyboard continues, and even in the US 21 states currently keep it on the public school curriculum. Champions of cursive writing point out studies that show it improves retention and comprehension as it engages the brain more deeply, improves fine motor skills, and primes the brain for increased learning. In lecture halls, students tend to take longer notes with the keyboard while those using pen and paper are more concise.

A research study with 12 7th graders and 12 adults in which brain waves were recorded while participants wrote the same note with a keyboard and with a digital pen proved that learning was better when students wrote or drew by hand (Swapna Krishna NOW, Nov 1, 2021).

While texting on digital devices is booming, creative writing is on the decline. A survey by the National Literacy Trust says that 14% of young people (between 14-16 years) write outside of school and homework and only 36% say they write if they had a choice. These low statistics seem to indicate that young people do not consider texting or posting on social media as creative writing. Encouraging your teen to put their thoughts on paper or a screen can be therapeutic given the increasing rates of mental health amongst the young. Five to ten minutes of writing per day expressing their feelings has been found to have a positive effect.

Cyber slang in texting and social media messaging is impacting writing, vocabulary, punctuation, and grammar, specifically capitalization and sentence formation. This impacts academic performance by shifting language style to casual from formal.

Public speaking improves overall communication skills and builds self-esteem. Some teens take to it naturally, while others are fearful and shy. It is an essential skill for leadership and career development, so it is worthwhile learning and mastering it from an early age. Poetry, drama, and singing help in overcoming stage fright, and you can also encourage your teen by helping them research and prepare a speech for their grade or school. If your teen shows talent, they may like to join a Toastmasters International Gavel club or a debating club. Watching movies like *The King's Speech*, *Kids President*, or *Larry Crowne* with your teen could help in picking up the tips and tricks of public speaking.

Chapter 9:

Managing Yourself

All creatures eat, but man only dines. –Mrs. Beeton (Household Management).

Since its publication in 1851, Mrs. Beeton's handbook still remains contemporary with many of her recipes, and tips on cooking and dining appearing in more recent works. But it seems her rules for dining and table manners are being forgotten except perhaps at the high table of exclusive dining halls and expensive fine dining restaurants. Her bookmarked the epitome of a cultural shift to using cutlery and sitting in high-backed chairs from centuries of eating with your fingers in the middle ages. With the advent of fast food culture though it seems that the wheel has turned a full circle and sloppy medieval feasting has returned with "finger-lickin' good" chicken wings, drumsticks, burgers, and pizzas all eaten with your hands in a casual banquet in front of the TV. Table manners though should not be forgotten, since they still have the potential to shape family life because meals are a social ritual even as eating is a physical need.

Learning to feed themselves is the very first life skill a baby learns, and parents soldier on through many months of sloppy eating till their baby finally masters the necessary motor skills. Continuing this learning by teaching your child from an early age the correct way to hold and use cutlery in the right order, place settings, and dining etiquette–ladies and guests first being the order of serving, the difference between glass and crystalware is a good approach to sensitize them on social graces because mealtimes remain a regular feature of daily life as they grow up and thus offer an opportunity for reinforcing good habits and building their self-esteem.

It will give your teen confidence in social situations while establishing your authority and credibility as a source of information on social graces, making you the "go to" person for your teen. You will find this much less stressful than tolerating years of sloppiness at mealtime and attempting a crash course on etiquette and social graces in the three months between high school and college. If you want them to stop multitasking with screens during mealtimes, you will have to set an example by putting yours away too. You will also have to take the lead in appreciating family and maintaining family links by involving them in birthday celebrations, keeping in touch through visits or phone calls, maintaining family chat groups on social media and helping out in times of distress or need. Creating a family tree with your teen can be a fun way to teach them family history and help them identify relatives whom they meet less frequently.

Social Media Cuts Both Ways in Teen Friendships

Your teens may find it more difficult to retain old friends and make new ones during their teen years. Jealousy and peer pressure can cause friendships formed in elementary school to fray and it takes time to build trust in new friends. This has always been the norm for early teens but in today's "always on" world of social media, they are simultaneously pressured to have more friends than they can manage. A recent study published by Time magazine (October 14, 2022) says that teens feel pressured to expand their online social networks beyond the ideal network number that humans can manage (150) by the desire to "be nice" and not hurt anyone's feelings but they then are stressed by having to respond to a firehose of posts with speed of response seen as a test of friendship. This not only affects their attention span but results in shallower, less meaningful friendships.

Hobbies, Community Activity, and the Arts Help Unique Skills and Ripples of Friendship

Teens who take part in extracurricular activities are less likely to be open to risky behavior. Firstly, they have less time on their hands and next their peer group expands to include like-minded friends. Having a diverse group of friends also reinforces their self-confidence and self-esteem, making them more at ease in leadership. Encourage them to take on projects that showcase their abilities and develop talent. Acting, singing, debating, hip hop, ballet, social dancing, and public speaking are all great at teaching children to express themselves, manage body language and facial expression, speak clearly and project their voice, and use creativity and imagination. Overcoming stage fright at an early age is as important as learning to swim, cycle, or drive a car. A cookie sale fundraiser for a cause such as a flood relief, a meal for the homeless, or a treat for an elder's home is a simple but effective way to demonstrate caring for others and make empathy and kindness a habit. As a parent, you need to be open to encouraging them to plan, lending a hand, and even opening your wallet (since teens are not financially savvy their budgeting is always over-optimistic and in need of rescue). Every child is not a prodigy, but every child has a talent, and parents must consider it a primary responsibility to make that talent flourish even as formal education progresses because it is the combination of education and talent that makes a unique personality—the keystone of their success in adult life.

Chapter 10:

The Authentic Teen

We live in a decaying world. Young people no longer respect their parents. They are rude and impatient. They frequently inhabit taverns and have no self-control. –Inscription on an Ancient Egyptian tomb

Reconcile yourself to the fact that good behavior and early teens are like chalk and cheese. Throughout history, great philosophers like Socrates and writers like William Shakespeare have bemoaned the fact that teenagers are incorrigible. Previously, this behavior was thought to be due to the effect of raging hormones released during puberty. More recently, science has discovered a link to brain development as well. Using MRI scanners to investigate the teen brain, scientists have linked their behavior to how the brain changes during adolescence.

What science has established is that during adolescence, the neural pathways that link the different sections of the brain mature and strengthen at different speeds, and this starts progressively from the back of the brain to the front of it. In technical terms, the process starts from the amygdala and ends with the prefrontal cortex. The amygdala is the center of emotions, while the prefrontal cortex is the center of logic, decision-making, problem-solving, and controlling impulses.

In early adolescence, the amygdala is thus overactive and emotions rule till maturity brings in control and stability in the adult years researchers at the University of California estimate this to be nearer to 25 years. Is this then an evolutionary trick to annoy parents? Not quite, it seems. Rather, it is evolution preparing teens to take the risk of leaving the nest, as well as sharpening the fight-or-flight response to improve their chances of survival in the dangers lurking outside. Since our ancestors were hunter-gatherers working in tribes, we may have to assume that they were thus ready to apprentice and learn while preparing to take on greater responsibilities of family life later on.

Courtesy Is Never Out of Fashion

As humans evolve, it is the tribe that protects the young while they learn to fend for themselves. In modern times, it is the family that is at the core of this tribe plus co-opted members like grandparents, friends, neighbors, and teachers. Parents, however, have the prime role of setting the expected standard of behavior for their teens. This starts well before the early teen years when parents are the primary playmates of the toddler and sympathetic confidants of the pre-teen. Good manners, saying "please" and "thank you," respecting the views of elders, sharing, and not hurting others with words or actions are all learned at home by following your example. At this stage of their lives, you need to ease up on over-correcting your teen. You will get better results by supporting them in exploring their teen world while letting them feel your constant support and concern for their well-being.

What About Birth Order and Sibling Rivalry?

It is still not conclusively proved that birth order has an impact on personality type. Early research seemed to suggest that firstborns were more conscientious while lastborns were more adventurous. Other research suggests that firstborns have an IQ advantage of between one and two points, attributed to having the undivided attention of their parents as a baby, whereas children born later had to compete for attention with them. This advantage in IQ was, however, not seen to be significant in later adult years. However, observational research may permit us to be aware that firstborns tend to occupy a more favorable position while growing up and may even act more entitled, leading to arguments and conflict with their younger siblings. In some families, this could be more noticeable due to cultural norms—respecting the elder for example. Teenagers wanting more time on their own may resent younger siblings' constant need for attention while parents worry that the teens' neglect of household chores and refusal to tidy up their room could be setting a bad example. Resolving such issues without open conflict makes life tougher for already stressed and overworked parents.

Sibling rivalry—conflict between brothers and sisters or even younger and older children is common yet difficult to manage without being seen to favor one child over the other or the expectation that when provoked your intervention will save them. Constant conflict can be annoying, but it is best for a parent to not intervene unless there is a danger of escalation to physical violence. Children model their behavior on their parents. Having a mutually respectful relationship with your partner, managing your inevitable disagreements and arguments in private, being considerate of their needs and wants, listening to your significant other and showing appreciation of their opinion even if it differs from yours and generally having a bit of fun can be your biggest contribution in their lives. It makes your home a safe harbor from which teens can sail forth to explore and conquer new worlds.

Coping With Violence in Society

The United States is unique in having the highest rate of single-parent households in the world—23% according to Pew Research, and the third highest divorce rate in the world.

Is gun violence in the US the result of lax gun control laws that permit the purchase of long guns and high-capacity magazines (weapons that did not exist when the founding fathers enshrined "the right of the people to keep and bear arms" in the US Constitution), or is it a symptom of a mental health crisis? The US has 120.5 guns per 100 population. The US CDC reported that in 2020 of the 45,222 deaths due to firearms, the majority–24,292 were suicides and 19,384 were homicides. The rise in homicides, however, was 34% above the previous year and a 75% increase over 10 years. Mass shootings which get wide coverage in news media accounted for 1024 deaths and 1828 injuries. But they are on the rise and 2022 seems to be heading towards setting a new record in incidents of mass shootings despite the passing of a bi-partisan gun control act, which includes record Federal funds to States for enforcement.

With more guns in homes, children are experiencing firearms in the home, and gun-related injuries and incidents involving children are on the rise. Children are also subject to the mental and emotional trauma of school shootings and reports say that 75% of them are worried about a mass shooting incident happening in their own school rather than trying to focus on their education.

The United Kingdom has some of the strictest gun laws in the world resulting in knives being the weapon of choice for criminals and gangs. UK police recorded 49,027 incidents involving knives in the year to March 2021 and a 32% increase in sexual offenses including the highest recorded number of incidents of rape (ons.gov.uk, Nov. 2022). A September 2020 study by BMC Public Health on the Risk Factors Associated with Knife Crime in the UK reported that 30% of teenagers 11-13 would be carrying a knife. The same study found that strong parental attachment was a protective factor and conflicts with parents increased victimization and offending.

So, how do parents respond to their children in explaining violence? The American Psychiatric Association and The American Academy of Pediatrics recommend avoiding the topic altogether till around eight years if it does not directly affect your family because the child will struggle to process it.

Their advice in delivering any bad news to children of any age is to first get your own reaction under control, preferably in private. With a child under six, a one-sentence story based on your beliefs is best. You could also change the conversation by talking about the positives or the heroes. For elementary school children, the recommendation is to shield them from seeing pictures because the images will stay in their minds longer than words. If they do see pictures, try to erase them with positive photographs. With Tweens start by asking them if they have heard the news and asking how they feel. Use the opportunity to share your beliefs and have a conversation about your values. Make the conversation about your child rather than the event. You can use this same approach with Teens but expect them to challenge you about your activism on this issue. It is an opportunity for you to set an example to your children that when something is wrong, they need to fix it. Involving your teen in working towards change makes them resilient and aware.

Chapter 11:
Emotional Energy

Even with your best efforts to maintain a stable home, teens can worry about home life. More often than not, they will surprise you with school assignments or party invitations at very short notice accompanied by the need to shop for supplies or a new outfit and gift, and if you have made other plans, you might not react well. This will begin to make them anxious that they could lose face with their friends or study group. Because you have made them feel confident, they have, almost by default, taken on the leadership role and now they feel you are not supporting them. Your plans as far as your teen is concerned, is not the priority. So, this is going to cause stress in the home and for a few days, you are literally walking on eggshells.

Curfews, chores, or household responsibilities can cause them to worry. You have involved them in family budgeting, and they begin to worry if family finances are stable enough to support their future college education. You discuss work-life issues and the economy, and they start thinking about what would happen if you lose your job. When they take part in sports, they can experience disappointment and frustration if they do not make the team, the team loses, or the coach is no good.

With so much social media and celebrities peddling brands, teens can suffer from a low self-image. Peer pressure can make them stressed about fitting in. A lower-than-expected grade can impact their self-esteem. Fear of failure is always lurking in their minds, even though they may rarely express it. Securing a place in a good college, aspiring to enter the same college as their closest friends, and the choice of a major or career are all likely to make them anxious. And teens do not think in a logical sequence which means that they could be stressing out about something that is a year or two away in your timeframe.

Transition From Playmate to Role Model

Now what happens is that being typical teens they will try to hide their worries from you. You might not even realize that they are experiencing stress from the few brief daily conversations that you have with them. Even though you have made being transparent and open a priority since the time they started talking they may still have worry and anxiety that are not shared with you. Thus, you need to be constantly on the lookout for telltale signs that suggest your teen needs help or reassurance. Be ready always to jump into their world and listen to their problems, however trivial or small they may seem to you. Be on the lookout for signs that your teen may be bullied or unwittingly being a bully in school. Sometimes teens are triggered by seemingly inconsequential behavior. A friendship that seems over, not being invited to a party, an uncooperative teammate, an upcoming assignment, or a module test can stress even a well-adjusted teen. Just talking things over can be the tonic they need to move on from overthinking their problem.

Home should be a place of comfort, serenity, and warmth, positively impacting comfort and safety. A place for nurturing, love, consideration, and care. While routine may help in arranging the best use of family time, be on the lookout for breakout activities that can create fun and break monotony and boredom. Inviting family or friends over for a potluck meal, a weekend barbeque, or bringing a dish party, a movie night or a stage play, or a concert can be impromptu activities that create family togetherness. Be open to your teen's suggestions and preferences too.

Share Family Time and Expose Your Teen to Spirituality

Weekend trips can be an opportunity for family time and bonding especially if the family has been busy with their individual priorities for some time. A hike is a good way to connect with nature while camping out is useful for reconnecting with basic living and survival skills. Adventure parks and trails help build confidence.

Early teens are also a good time for exposure to activism and supporting causes. It helps them develop an understanding of local and global issues that will affect their future while also allowing them to build new connections and friendships. If they have an underdeveloped talent, this is an opportunity to let it blossom in a nonjudgmental space.

The more active your teen is the less likely they are to be drawn into risky peer groups. Spirituality is now more popular than organized religion. Parents should bring their children into their spiritual practice just so that they understand the concepts and rituals. Exploring spirituality in greater depth should be a decision left for the young adult rather than the early teen.

Should you practice meditation or yoga, introduce your teen to the basic light exercises that can help control breathing and manage emotional reactions. Yoga is an amazingly beneficial practice based on combining stretching and breath control. Most people, however, are put off by the almost mystical approach that is taught by its master practitioners. And the many hours of practice necessary under the guidance of expert yogis before you can master the asanas (poses) and pranayama (breath control). The novice yogi can then progress to non-attachment to the material values of normal life, developing the skills of concentration and meditation and ultimately reaching the goal of a trancelike state of bliss. This is thus a lifelong learning process that only the most ardent disciples proceed with. There is also the cost in terms of money and time in attending 14-day retreats and weekend refresher sessions to keep you motivated.

The golden hour before sunrise and sunset is particularly auspicious for yoga or meditation practice because it is the time when nature awakens and closes down and thus perfect for consciousness and nature to meet. We know that both practices come from the East—the Sanskrit word for sunrise or sunset is "sandhya" and combines "san" meaning "good" and "dhya," "to meditate." Teens need plenty of sleep during their adolescent years, are not early risers, and a heavy school day followed by extracurricular activity and homework is likely to leave them exhausted by evening. Family vacations are probably the best times to initiate them into either of these practices. Not only do you have more control over their routine during a holiday, but many locations lend themselves to a heightened spirituality through their peaceful, scenic nature.

Exercise and Fitness—Keep It Simple

Simple stretching exercises though, based on the yoga principles are an alternative to traditional yoga practice, and their increased popularity is linked to the lockdowns of the COVID-19 pandemic as people looked to counter the ill effects of isolation and the hours spent hunched over a laptop while Working From Home (WFH). Stretching helps you look good with a toned body while improving flexibility and has mood-boosting benefits too. Stretching does not require you to dress fashionably in athletic leisure wear and you only need loose-fitting comfortable clothing. Neither does it require expensive equipment- a kitchen chair for support, if necessary, a mat to prevent feet from slipping, and the space to swing your arms or lie flat is all that is needed along with a positive frame of mind. Six Minute Morning Stretching by Faye Rowe has easy-to-follow step-by-step instructions and a basic two-week plan for a supple body and relaxed mind. The only extra equipment you need is a good alarm clock to wake you up six minutes earlier than usual.

You cannot force a child into either meditation or yoga because it needs a very relaxed mind and body connectedness, and slowing down a teen mind is not an easy task. It is still very much driven by emotion rather than logic. The likelihood of early teens maintaining a regular practice of either is also unlikely but include them if you are a devotee of exercise and they may find it easier to come back to practice and improve their skills when they feel the need to slow the effects of aging in later life.

Reflexology, also known as Reflex Zone Therapy, is a non medicinal treatment that is believed to have originated in India and China as acupressure therapy over 5,000 years ago. However, it is more definitively linked to Egyptian civilization through a hieroglyphic found on the 4,500-year-old tomb of a king's physician. Native American tribes too practiced acupressure and US President James Garfield (1881) used acupressure on different points of his feet to reduce the pains of an assassination attempt when pain medication gave him no relief. Dr. William Fitzgerald (1872-1942) is credited with working to rediscover reflexology through his work at Central London ENT Hospital and the Boston City Hospital.

The theory behind acupressure is that it uses pressure on specific spots on the body which are believed to be linked to the internal organs and pressing on them stimulates their well-being. Bioenergy is thought to flow through meridians in the body and pressure on points found on the hands, feet, and ears is used to make the flow smooth and harmonious, thus improving the functioning of the organs. Dr. Fitzgerald's work focused on the feet and his success influenced others to map the entire human body into five longitudinal and four transverse zones on the soles of the two feet. This popularized foot reflexology as a treatment to stimulate the immune system, strengthen the body's natural resistance and eliminate toxins from the system. It can relieve most common aches, and pains and restore bodily functions such as temperature, blood pressure, heart rate, respiratory rate, and acidic-alkaline balance while creating a sense of well-being and relaxation if combined with a balanced diet, regular exercise and avoiding excessive use of stimulants.

Although reflexology is normally given using pressure from the thumb and fingers on specific zones on the soles and ankles, the daily use of a foot roller for three to five minutes is a convenient way to get the benefit of a general treatment of the whole body. Using a foot roller is an easy way to cover all spots related to the internal organs and restore balance. Thus, keeping a foot roller under a workspace or study table is a fun way to help your body stay healthy and your teen will likely enjoy this too.

Chapter 12:

First Taste of Freedom

The term "latchkey kids" was common in the '70s and early '80s—with mom and dad both at work or divorced, children would let themselves into their homes after school, fix a snack, do their homework, go out to play or have a friend come over. Although the term is not commonly used today, it is estimated that 11 million children (20% of the student population in the US) are still latchkey kids (HowStuffWorks 2017, June, 12). A big difference though is that the Gen Zs of 40 years ago were from higher income families while the latchkey kids of today are from low-income families, with parents possibly juggling multiple jobs.

Many Gen Zs have responded to their own "free range" childhood by vowing to spare their children the experience of the loneliness and worry they felt when parents were late to get home or they fell off the bike with none to tend to their injury. The result of this is that the pendulum has swung the other way with "helicopter parenting." Parents of today's generation are constantly hovering around their kids and telling them what they should do.

The Temptation to Overparent Is Overpowering

Two educational researchers interviewed 300 latchkey kids in 1982 for People Magazine and found that at least one-third of them reported suffering from high fear and recurring nightmares due to parents coming home late. But then, 35 years on, as adults they look back and value the freedom and trust that they experienced in their childhood. Julie Lythcott-Haimes, a free-range kid from the '80s based her book *How to Raise an Adult: Break Free of the Overparenting Trap and Prepare Your Kids for Success* on her experiences as the Dean of Freshmen at Stanford University. She found that many of her students from upper-middle class families had high test scores and grades and a long list of extra activities, but they could not think for themselves and solve a simple problem without consulting their parents which she says is a result of today's over parenting style.

Lenore Skenazy is the daughter of a stay-at-home mother who gave her the freedom to walk home from school at an early age and spend unstructured and unsupervised free time. Her mission is to combat the parent hysteria that children left alone today are in constant danger. When her son Izzy was nine years, she took him to a Manhattan department store and left him with instructions on how to find his way home on the subway. Writing about his experience about a month later, she found her story dominating every news channel the next day and was at the receiving end of a storm of protest over bad parenting and labeled "America's Worst Mother". She responded to this by writing a book with advice and forming the organization "Free Range Kids." One of her later initiatives was to dedicate a day to "Take your kids to the park and leave them alone." As expected, this raised a storm of controversy too with parents predicting a field day for pedophiles. But in an interview with an Australian news channel ABC News on the sidelines of "The Festival of Dangerous Ideas" in Sydney, she claimed that although the crime was actually declining in most States, parent hysteria is fed by three factors—increased sensationalism in the 24-hour cable news cycles, society becoming more litigious and everyone thinking like lawyers, and the "kiddie safety industrial complex." This last one, Skenazy says, has given rise to so many absurd and unnecessary products, quoting the example of 10,000 items in "Babies R Us" stores. In her book she also refers to the example of "Sesame Street" to drive home the point of how things have changed—PBS released a retrospective video collection "Sesame Street Old School," a set of its episodes broadcast from the mid-'70s to the early '80s with a warning "For Adult Viewing Only," because it features children playing unsupervised.

You Are the Best Judge of Your Teen's Ability

So, at what age do parents think it safe to send their children out unsupervised? Most agree that it is in the early teen years— between 11 and 13 and depending on whether they feel their kids are ready. But before they do, parents should teach their kids some basics– how to cross the road safely, how to contact them in an emergency, whom to contact as plan B if for any reason their parents do not respond immediately in an emergency, how to cycle safely, the common public transport routes to use, how to swim, how to contact emergency services.

Gun violence in the US overshadows the fact that the crime rate is declining except in a few cities. This probably influences US parents to be extra protective of young children, but they can learn from customs and cultures from around the world because parental love is universal, and re-examine what good parenting looks like. Elementary school children in Japan would most often use public transport or walk to school and in the safety of the school be given responsible tasks like cleaning the school including the bathrooms and serving lunch to classmates. The Japanese TV show *My First Errand* featuring children aged two to five undertaking tasks like shopping has been popular for decades although it only became popular in the US following its release on Netflix this year.

In Scandinavian countries like Denmark, parents park their babies in strollers outside cafes because of the cultural belief that fresh air helps babies sleep better and is healthier too. You could see babies sleeping in strollers outside homes and daycare centers, as well as bars, shops, and restaurants. In America though, leaving a child in a car even briefly or sending them to a local playground by themselves may result in the parents being reported to the authorities. In 1997 a visiting Danish mother who left her baby in a pram outside a New York City restaurant while having a drink with her partner inside was arrested and lost custody of her daughter temporarily.

Enlist Your Extended Family and Friends

In many countries, there is a collective approach to caregiving with the extended family supporting the mother so she could attend to other obligations without thinking that not staying at home with them constantly harms the child's development or attachment. In contrast, in the US you see a trend to exclusive parenting, with an every-nuclear-family-to-itself approach.

Like many things in life, being safe outside the home cannot be taught through one-dimensional paper-based learning. It is best remembered through experiential learning using all our human senses in the reality of a 3D world. A family trip to the city, shopping mall, fun fair, or museum, by subway or bus, gives kids the opportunity to learn about public transport and be confident even if their regular mode of travel is by car. An interstate plane trip, a river cruise, or a boating expedition can be a fun experience while being educational too. Bringing up kids outdoors is a wonderful bonding experience for busy families and an opportunity to learn about nature and the environment. While Google maps and travel blogs have all but made guidebooks redundant, map reading, and compass bearings are still the most basic techniques for surviving outdoors when technology fails. Observing the movement of the sun during the day and, if you live in the northern hemisphere, the North star at night are simple navigational skills to learn. Landmarks in the city and suburbs in relation to home or a parent's workplace are essential references. All of this builds confidence in your child that they can be safe in an unexpected emergency even in today's GPS tracking world.

The key to being confident with allowing your teen to "free range" in daily life of course is to be aware of where they are likely to be, with whom, and how they plan to spend that time. If your teen is spending time with friends, then it would be normal for you to expect the parents of the friend who initiated the activity to play the role of the backstop. It is always a good idea to let your teen know that their freedom is limited to circles of peers whom you know. These circles can be schools, societies, sports, neighbors, extended family, or study groups.

Chapter 13:

Life-Saving Skills

Swim instructors say a child is ready to learn when they are able to stand with their nose above the waterline in a baby pool. Generally, this would be by age four and start with learning to float, tread water and move toward safety. Many children who start at this age have by age five have mastered freestyle swimming (also known as the front crawl). If either parent can swim and you have access to a public pool you could play the role of an instructor under the watchful eye of a lifeguard. Spending more time in the water consistently is the best way for a child to learn to swim. And school vacations or family holidays can be used to teach or improve swimming through fun activities in the pool. Hiring a coach is expensive and even if affordable, learning just through regular lessons is slower unless the child is able to swim between lessons, too.

Catch Them Young

When your child is learning to swim, focus on the basics. The first step is to learn to be comfortable and relaxed in the water. This is because a swimmer has to fill their lungs with air to stay afloat. Being relaxed supports filling the lungs with long breaths, unlike the short sharp breathing when excited. The next step is for them to learn to float on their back. Using a life jacket helps when learning although it should not become a regular prop. Beginners learn to paddle swim (also known as the doggie crawl) and then how to swim underwater while controlling their breathing. Finally, they need to learn how to jump in and exit the pool. This gives them the confidence to stay calm if they should accidentally fall into a pool or a large body of water. Once they have learned these five basic steps you can help them improve speed and distance through pool play through games such as swim tag. Similar to freeze tag played indoors or in your backyard but remember to set the boundaries within the pool depth so that your child is safe. Remember that swimming in places where a lifeguard is on hand is best and remind your child especially to do so if you are not with them.

Some parents believe learning to swim even earlier—at age two or three is possible but experts caution that toddlers develop the necessary mental capacity only around five. Swimming, like cycling, is a skill that once learned is never forgotten.

Swimming is a great aerobic exercise that unlike running, racquet games and contact sports does not have long-term effects on the joints while a typical swimmer's body with broad shoulders, flat belly, toned muscles, and low body fat is coveted as an ideal of beauty in many cultures. Of course, this runs counterintuitive to the fact that having body fat helps a swimmer float more easily.

Lifesaving and CPR Are Useful Emergency Rescue Skills

Learning essential lifesaving skills as a teen is also possible assuming they have already learned to swim. The Red Cross organization offers training and certification, and the Boy Scouts Association and Girl Guides have proficiency badges in lifesaving while the International Lifesaving Federation has member organizations across the world.

Rescuing a person who is drowning is risky and many would-be rescuers have drowned in the process too as panic causes a person who is drowning to grip the rescuer and restrict their ability to swim while pulling them to safety or stand on the would-be rescuer in a desperate attempt to reach for air. Teach your teen that should they see signs of distressed swimming–gasping for air, a weak stroke, hands waving from side to side, swimming against a current, vertical in the water with no leg movement or with head thrown back and mouth wide open, or floating face down, they should first call 911 and give the exact location or alert another person before attempting a rescue. The golden rule of rescue is to reach, throw, row, or go.

out

a

pole

or

branch

for

the

person

t

m
a
h
u
m
a
n

c
h
a
i
n

i
f

a

s
u
f
f
i
c
i
e
n
t

n
u
m
b
e

a
v
e
r

o
r

a

r
o
p
e

t
o

t
h
e

p
e
r
s
o
n

i
n

d
i
s
t
r

- Go tie a rope around your waist an

l you out of the water if necessary.

Basic first aid once the person drowning is out of the water (if unconscious and no one has witnessed the incident always assume when handling that a neck injury is possible).

In cold weather remove all clothes, and cover with a blanket. Watch for signs of hypothermia.

Look for signs of choking by food, debris, or tongue folding back, and clear the trachea with your fingers.

Check for pulse and begin modified CPR if there are no signs of breathing. Place hands on the center of the chest and push hard and fast–about 2 per second. They should not attempt rescue breathing (mouth-to-mouth resuscitation) unless properly trained because there are concerns about negative effects if cardiac arrest has occurred.

Swimming Opens the Door to Watersports and Exploration

If your child shows an interest in pursuing swimming as a sport, you may want to enroll them in the school swim team. Even schools that do not have their own pool have access to public pools for team training. They can then progress to learning swim styles and strokes and work towards achieving competitive timing and even participation in other aquatic sports such as diving, water polo, and synchronized swimming.

Rowing apart from being the most demanding sport in terms of muscle strength and endurance produces some of the fittest athletes in the world and has a well-deserved reputation of being an upper-middle to upper-class sport mainly because of the high cost of the Olympic-class sculls required to train and compete. Rowing though is the best sport to teach high-performance team skills. It requires total dedication, concentration, and focus on the end goal. You need to work on your individual skill of dropping the blade in the water at the perfect angle "the catch point" to deliver a perfectly coordinated smooth and powerful thrust to propel the boat. You might think that being the coxswain is easier because cox never row. But the cox carries the great responsibility of setting the right direction and coordinating the power and the timing of the rowers. And, if you want to cox you had better be a good swimmer because rowing tradition demands that the winning team throws their cox into the waters either at the end of the row or at the awards ceremony!

Being a good swimmer helps you to brave large bodies of water, be they oceans, lagoons, rivers or lakes and leads to other less competitive but fun activities such as paddleboarding, waterskiing, surfing, kite sailing, windsurfing, and scuba diving. As 71% of the Earth's surface is covered by water, the oceans may prove to be the new frontier for your future young adult to explore as expanding global populations crowd the land and reduce arable land available for food cultivation. The largely unexplored ocean's depths also hold rare natural resources needed to maintain industrial production.

Chapter 14:

Living in an "Always On" World

> ... *technology for Generation Alpha is not something separate from themselves, but rather, an extension of their own consciousness and identity.*
> –Natalie Franke, Head of Community, HoneyBook

Every generation struggles with the stress of standing out while fitting in. Gen Zs were probably the last generation to have to do this in the physical world–smart devices rolled out only when they were in their late teens. They were under pressure from their families to go to art, dance, or music lessons and faced far more pressure than previous generations to go to college—60% versus 48% of millennials whose parents expected them to attend college according to The American National Family Survey 2021 quoted by The Survey Center on American Life in a recent storyline. Thus, Gen Zs are considered to be the loneliest generation yet—56% responded by saying they felt lonely and isolated. Parents of the Alpha generation (today's teenagers) thus face an even greater challenge in preparing their children to stand out as leaders while not making them feel isolated and prone to depression and mental health issues. The answer lies in building strong communities that foster social ties—a practice from the past which has been overlooked in the parental dream of raising overachievers.

The First Generation to Be Born Connected

Technology was a tool for millennial parents. For Gen Alpha though, technology is a way of life. The first iPad was launched in 2010 just as they were born and so too was the first version of Instagram which their parents soon adopted for "sharenting"—sharing baby pictures and family life. Fittingly, perhaps, Alpha's are also known as the "glass generation"— rapidly adapting to doing everything through screens and experiencing firsthand the 4th. The industrial revolution is driven by Artificial Intelligence (AI), Machine Learning, The Internet of Things (IoT), and the Metaverse.

This convergence of the internet, smart devices, and social media apps are helping Gen Alpha to both standout and fit in too. This has also freed them to pursue unconventional career paths with the lure of becoming "kidfluencers" and making millions even before thinking of college and careers. From Japan's Coco PinkPrincess to the Fashionista twin models from Brazil raising money for their father's leukemia treatment, social media influencers have raised millions by unboxing and reviewing toys, fashion trends, and beauty products too for their millions of followers. Some have made a career out of activism like Little Miss Flint a 13-year-old who fights against water contamination in Central Michigan, USA, and Kyle Giersdorf who made $4 million by winning an eSports championship. Their careers are managed by savvy parents whose own careers in dance, fashion, or just happenstance posting of unboxing gifts or pet pictures launched their teens' careers.

Opening Doors, Closing Minds

The internet and social media are thus a two-edged sword that can bring fame and fortune or just create additional stress for teens through intense peer pressure to be always connected and responding to posts and messages from an ever-ballooning network of friends and friends of friends. Failure to respond immediately to even the most mundane messages can be taken as signs of indifference and cause friendships to be questioned. At the same time, being left out of parties or social meets and seeing these pictures on social media streams intensifies loneliness and stress too. Teens are thus struggling to manage an expanding network of virtual friends while screens replace physical meetings making them feel lonelier than previous generations. This places more responsibility on the family to step up and provide balance through interaction and activities.

The one constant you can be certain of is that it is impossible to turn back the clock on change. The predictable linear patterns of behavior and approaches to problem-solving of past generations are giving way to more agile approaches to decision-making and finding solutions. One major impact that is already being researched is the effect Google has on education. In the past when knowledge resided in books memory learning was the standard that defined dedicated learners. Rote learning and memorization are giving way to "digital amnesia"—information is not committed to memory when it is readily available through internet search engines like Google. While this has democratized education by making information accessible to everyone irrespective of social or economic class it can also be illusory in that the quality of that information may be subjective. The rise of fake news, bots, and trolls point to this growing menace.

Short Attention Spans, Quick to Fail and Recover

This brings up the subject of critical thinking skills which we discuss in the next chapter. But in the rest of this chapter let us discuss how decision-making has changed in the knowledge economy. The agile behavior that Gen Z has already adopted can be summarized as—Iterate, Learn, and Evolve. As with education, the internet has changed research too. Not only is there more access to current thinking and analysis, but it also makes information gathering through surveys easier too through programs like Survey Monkey. A simpler example—if your teen wants to decide between watching *Squid Games* and *Stranger Things* they could poll their peer group through WhatsApp, Telegram, Viber, or Snapchat and have answers within minutes. Or they could look up a review on YouTube or TikTok. In your teen years you would probably have asked your mom for permission to use the telephone and called up a friend or two at most whom you knew were fans of *Rugrats*, *Arthur*, or *The Brady Bunch*.

What smart devices and the internet do is make insight gathering easier. And this means that your teen can not only make a decision based on that information or even build a model faster, but they can also modify or trash it quicker too because the cost of being wrong is a low bar. So, they can create a "minimum viable product" and keep learning and evolving their project continuously. Two generations of Tech entrepreneurs provide the contrast to understand this better. Both Bill Gates and Steve Jobs invested significant time, energy, money, and people in building Microsoft and Apple. And their organizations continue to do so today to stay ahead of the competition. Contrast this with Larry Page and Mark Zuckerberg who founded Google and Facebook respectively while still in university on the simple idea of finding information more easily by ranking pages (Google) and connecting Harvard students (Facebook). Each of these founders was solving a problem common to their circle of friends and fellow students–their tribe which rapidly resonated globally. Google is now a global powerhouse that is outmaneuvering Microsoft and Apple in education through Google-powered low-cost Chromebook laptops and Apps. In this process, Google has influenced a curriculum change from traditional academic knowledge like math formulas to training children in using skills like problem-solving and teamwork. This is changing the role of education too from producing skilled workers to developing knowledgeable citizens.

Chapter 15:

Critical Thinking

"An idea is a bisociation of two previously unconnected thoughts." –Miles Young. Warden, New College, Oxford and former Chairman, Ogilvy Worldwide

Honestly, it is difficult to imagine that parents would need to wait to teach problem-solving and critical thinking till their children are reaching early adolescence. It would be the worst time to do this with emotional development racing ahead of logical thought and teens pushing back at parental authority to assert independence and freedom. Any responsible parent would want their child to grow up to be a socially well-adjusted adult with good physical and mental abilities. This would be the common goal of generations of parents. But what has changed is parenting styles.

Today's parents want to be seen as "cool" and thus adopt an inclusive and permissive style and in trying to be friends rather than parents they are reluctant to enforce rules and discipline in the home. But in doing this they lose respect and authority. If you think back to your own childhood, you will recall that parents then were firm in setting rules in the home but also warm and caring at the same time. This authoritative parenting style created obedience and respect which carried through to college and work life.

Encourage Diversity

The way we think guides how we work. Ned Herrmann who led management education at General Electric (GE), conducted research that led to the concept of whole-brain thinking which he perfected over 40 years and with 2 million leaders and managers worldwide. His whole-brain thinking model represents the different thinking preferences that are demonstrated by people and organizations and are divided into four quadrants—Rational, Intuitive, Theoretical, and Realistic. Each of these quadrants is equally important, displays individual traits, and is available to everyone. While the tools and platform of the whole brain model are certainly too advanced for home use, the concept can be borrowed by parents to understand their own thinking style and that of their teens. Accommodating a diversity of thinking styles in the family not only brings greater harmony to the home but also equips your teens with a self-awareness that builds confidence as they grow into young adults and take on greater responsibilities.

Treat Play Seriously

Thinking back to your childhood again, you may remember that learning through play was part of the daily routine–whether indoor games or outdoor fun, games taught creativity, problem-solving, and critical thinking skills. Music, from a very early age, is also associated with cognitive development especially classical music which has a complex structure that helps in neural development from zero to three years. Nursery rhymes introduce children to storytelling and promote social skills while being a foundation for reading and spelling. Reading encourages creativity because words build pictures in the mind. Remind yourself that all great inventions that have built the world we live in today, including the internet, space travel, and even the metaverse were built by entrepreneurs and scientists whose creativity was inspired by reading. Their screen time watching television or the cinema was limited.

Buddy parents using screens as a "timepass" activity are leading children from a very early age to live more sedentary lives and increasing their risk of Non-Communicable Diseases (NCD) like Type 2 diabetes and obesity. Even if you live far from a beach, a simple sandbox introduces the child to textures while giving them an independent play experience that contributes to building trust and confidence through casual separation that reduces separation anxiety and promotes healthy attachment with your child. Of course, if you can make a trip to the beach, using a small shovel and truck to build a sandcastle helps in fine motor skills development while burying themselves in the sand gives children a sense of their body relative to space. Sandplay also encourages children to learn to share by accomplishing a goal like building a sandcastle together while sharing tools and toys. While being outdoors, climbers help a child's physical development such as hand and foot coordination, balance, and agility while helping develop directional awareness.

The isolation of COVID-19 lockdowns sparked new adult interest in an old favorite—jigsaw puzzles. They have always remained useful toys for building motor skills, hand-eye coordination, visual perception, memory, comprehension, improved attention span, and concentration as well as problem-solving from toddler upwards. Completing a puzzle gives a sense of achievement which grows with attempting and solving more complex jigsaws such as 1000 and 5000-piece puzzles.

Crosswords, Sudoku, Nintendo Brain Age, the Rubix cube, and strategy games like Mastermind, Minesweeper, Backgammon, Chess, draughts, carrom, and table tennis, are great for when your toddler turns into a tween. Lego still tops the list of toys with the potential to teach a wide range of skills ranging from problem-solving, creativity, experimentation, teamwork, communication, and self-confidence.

Use Everyday Situations to Open Minds

Hobbies too can be fun while they help develop your child's mind and keep them occupied. Gardening, art, photography, stamp collecting, numismatics, learning to play the piano, guitar, or violin. Singing, hip hop, or ballet, are good if you have the time to arrange and accompany your child to practice sessions or can arrange a reliable chaperone. Even involving your child in a regular discussion of current affairs and local and global issues builds a child's thinking and problem-solving skills and activism expands social contacts and friendships. Vacation time, specifically the long summer holidays, is ideal to start an activity when your regular routine and schoolwork restrict the time you can spend with your child. Summer camps focus on STEM activities, outward-bound programs, and community-based leadership training. Short courses are ways to pull your child out of a sedentary lifestyle and into the active outdoors.

In developing critical thinking and problem-solving skills your own ingenuity is your best resource and looking for opportunities and examples in daily life is a simple but effective path forward. While screens will remain a fact of life, be open to every opportunity to point to real-life events and examples to keep your teens grounded in the practical realities of life and open to common-sense solutions.

Chapter 16:
Problem Solving

Too often we give our children answers to remember rather than problems to solve. –Roger Lewin Ph.D. Biochemist, former deputy editor, New Scientist.

Most advice on problem-solving skills stems from 70s research and approaches the topic from a logical adult point of view. There are four-step, eight-step, and 12-step processes that recommend linear approaches based on problem definition and clarification, determining root causes, ranking causes in order of importance, and developing an action plan.

But how much of this is relevant to today's teen brain? Firstly, there is a vast amount of information on any topic available at their fingertips. Then there are social media– sharing experiences, reviews, advice, warnings, and tips on every issue of interest to friends and connections. The internet makes them more easily distracted and reduces their ability to ignore distractions. Data Science and AI try to analyze and interpret data to make decision-making informed and simplified. Google has put forward a new concept called the "messy middle" which is based on tracking user data on their platform to track consumer behavior and challenges traditional linear approaches to consumer decision-making.

Stop Chasing Rainbows

In helping your teen improve problem-solving skills it is best to stay rooted in encouraging them through the tools already available in education. Reading is important to gather information and ideas, but writing improves comprehension by teaching the importance of filtering out what is irrelevant in the text and connecting it to the real world. Comprehension refers to your ability to understand and have clarity of thought. Writing is much easier now with the keypad and smartphone replacing pen and paper. Writing by hand though has added benefits because it opens the brain up to learning and remembering according to a 2020 study by the Norwegian University of Science and Technology (NTNU) published in Frontiers in Psychology. While the digitization of education is taking place at a faster pace, as a parent you may have to play a bigger role in encouraging the use of handwritten essays and stories in the pre-teen years for your child to benefit from the best of both worlds. You could also consider investing in a digital pen and installing a writing App on their tablet or smartphone.

Mathematics is another subject in the educational curriculum that promotes resourcefulness, the ability to think logically and critically, and creativity all of which improve problem-solving skills. And since math is the foundation of computer logic, it is essential for programming and computer science. Managing time and developing patience is also essential and contributes to developing better social and situational awareness. Parents thus have the opportunity to tackle the concepts and process of problem-solving through practical approaches that are relevant to their teen.

Faster Is Not Necessarily Better

The role of technology in their lives though makes teens more vulnerable to heuristic thinking. Heuristics are mental shortcuts for solving problems quickly assuming the solution to be sufficient or useful when bound by the limited time available. While this does speed up decision-making, it can also lead to poor decisions due to using only limited data or facts. Heuristics is partly due to the evolutionary process meant to help our human brains handle the vast complexity of information, and problems large and small, that feed into our brains through our senses in our daily lives. But when your everyday decisions are fast, unconscious, and automatic they are error-prone too. Complex decisions are made slower, more thoughtfully, and with more effort are more likely to be reliable.

Decisions can be influenced by biases or mental habits like familiarity, availability, scarcity, trial, and error, anchoring, and confirmation. Confirmation bias for example leads you to ignore facts and evidence that do not support your beliefs and ideas while searching for and remembering those that do. Of all the biases, confirmation bias is the strongest and most pervasive. An example of how confirmation bias can affect your teen is the choice of media when you select news organizations and stories that validate your view of the world. Algorithms learn your preferences and you can soon be trapped in a filter bubble—a personal information ecosystem that feeds your existing beliefs and prevents you from getting information that could prove you wrong. This is the main reason why we accept "fake news."

You can help your teen recognize confirmation bias by helping them identify its symptoms. For example, when they are convinced they are right or experience strong emotions around a belief. Being open to being wrong and learning to separate your belief from your identity. Search for evidence that will prove you wrong when all your information sources are tuned to prove you right.

Overconfidence Is Not Expertise

Overconfidence can be the result of limited knowledge or competence which leads you to be unaware that you don't know but overrate your own knowledge and abilities. Your teen may see a lot of these on social media aggressively pushing their opinions. The solution to being an overconfident idiot is to be humble and curious. Teach your teen intellectual humility and recognize that if an answer to a problem appears to be so simple, but yet missed by experts on that subject, it is worth considering that your teen, or you, could be wrong.

COVID-19-induced lockdowns and WFH gave millennial parents an opportunity to share a common experience of living and working in a virtual world. Both education and work moved to Zoom, MS Teams, Slack, Google Chat, Canva, YouTube, Blackboard, Edmodo became the go-to platforms, and socializing moved to FaceBook, Instagram, TikTok, Twitter, WhatsApp, Telegram, Messenger and LinkedIn, Fiver, Upwork, and Freelancer became the online recruitment space for Digital Nomads as quit their regular 9–5 jobs in record numbers.

Mental Health Is a Roller Coaster Not a Doom Loop

Parents are experiencing an increase in mental health issues such as depression, overthinking, and anxiety which were previously thought to be more prevalent with teens with screens. Indoor Environment Quality (IEQ), food quality, physical exercise, and work-life balance were found to be the main influences although there were external factors such as age, income, job role, and education. One study found that families with teens experienced fewer issues due to their being able to help out with household chores, compared to families with babies or toddlers. This shared experience could sensitize more parents to being more open to signals of trouble and empathetic in helping teens address the social issues they commonly encounter—body image, eating disorders, social media, peer pressure, education, on-screen violence, bullying, alcoholism, romance, and drug use.

Chapter 17:

Goal Setting

A goal without a plan is just a wish. – Antoine de Saint-Exupery, French author, and aviation pioneer

Your teen will have many goals–getting high grades on a subject they like, making friends with a romantic crush, completing a project to get an extra line on their college application, passing an exam with high grades, getting into a sports team, or even staying healthier. Their approach toward achieving their goals could be conditioned by the social and cultural norms in the family. In a family that is governed by traditional social norms, there could be mechanisms in place such as habits, rituals, or practices that pull them back or push them towards achieving these goals. Maintaining their morale and persevering could be the main challenge.

In westernized societies, there is greater individual freedom since the push and pull of tradition and external authority has weakened and they are expected to act on their own to achieve their goals. They carry the burden on their shoulders of staying motivated, energized, and connected and taking action if they are stuck. But dreams and fantasies may not be enough and failing regularly can be demotivating. Just being formula-driven and SMART—Specific, Measurable, Achievable, Relevant, and Timely in setting goals does not guarantee success. Agreed that SMART goal setting is motivating and gives direction and focus. But remember that "achievable" and "relevant" depend on an honest analysis of strengths and weaknesses. Now, think about your adolescent early teens' minds—their front-brained logical thinking is lagging behind while emotional development is racing ahead. This sets them up to overestimate their capabilities and minimize or ignore the difficulties that may arise. They can then be easily discouraged or blame someone else (parents!) when the goal is not met.

OOPS Is the New SMART for Early Teens

But, at the same time goal setting is important for positive thinking. So, it is a skill that needs to be encouraged. How can parents help? Perhaps by being more conversational in approach and bringing common sense to the process. This is like installing a safety net so the trapeze artist can learn to swing fearlessly because the inevitable falls will not matter.

This is my process which I call **"OOPS,"** an early teen-friendly goal-setting hack– **Outcome, Obstacles, Plan, Succeed**.

Help your teen to be clear about the outcome of what they are wishing for themselves and understand what is holding them back from achieving it (obstacles), make a plan to overcome the obstacles, and celebrate their success. They should also be willing to sacrifice personal enjoyment if necessary to achieve the satisfaction of accomplishment.

For example, the outcome may be to improve their math grade in an upcoming examination but unexpectedly, on the evening before they could be invited to a party or movie by a friend. What advice would you give them as a parent? Going to the party will save them from losing face and friendships and the resultant stress that could impact their frame of mind at the examination and impact their grade anyway. Of course, if they do really want that grade very badly and their mind is focused on it then they will have the fortitude to endure the short-term impact of skipping that party. They may have some past experience of the likely reaction from their friend and peer group and be ready with a plan to manage the situation. If they are very confident in their preparation, they may go to the party and also do well on the exam.

Learning to Fail Is Better Than Failing to Learn

As a parent, your advice rests on how well you understand your teen's personality and goals. While it is important to let them know that you will support them in their decision, you should resist the temptation to be judgmental about the outcome. Recrimination in the home can be as damaging and impact self-confidence just as much as peer pressure does. When you show your teen that you respect their judgment, they are more likely to draw the right conclusions on their own based on the results of their action and be ready to recommit to achieving their dreams. And grow in confidence that when obstacles arise, they do not necessarily have to hold you back from fulfilling your wish if you can plan to overcome them.

Teaching teens to persevere in spite of setbacks is also a way to inspire them to solve problems and achieve their goals. Teaching them to adopt a growth mindset in which they understand that personal development is a process that involves learning, hard work, and persistence. Unlike the fixed mindset where they believe their abilities, intelligence or talent is innate or hereditary and hence they may just try to look smart all the time and avoid risks that may make them look dumb. Children in a growth mindset believe that everyone can get smarter if they work at it. A study that looked at the mindset and student performance of 15-year-olds in Chile found that those students who had a growth mindset were three times more likely than their peers to score within the top 20% on national achievement tests. Conversely, in the same study, students with a fixed mindset were four times more likely to score in the bottom 20% (Sager, 2021).

Encourage a Growth Mindset

Teachers too have to play a role in helping teens develop a growth mindset by helping them gain confidence through not grading every assignment, particularly at the beginning of a lesson, and grading for learning–the understanding of the task at hand rather than compliance to due dates and formatting. Parents can encourage their teens that all minds do not need to work the same way and you need to value that some minds work differently. Teaching teens to develop a growth vocabulary through games and activities that focus on Captain Yes and Pirate Nope. Help them to set achievable goals and avoid overpraising their intelligence. Encourage them to take challenges and support them to take risks and accept that it is OK to fail sometimes.

Help your teen set up a growth mindset bulletin board for a sport, hobby, or activity, and use the language of a growth mindset to track daily progress while acknowledging that failure is a part of growing and moving forward. Look for posters with growth mindset quotes from your teen's favorite sports stars and role models and put them up in their den or bedroom. Encourage them to keep a journal. Journaling helps track goals while improving writing skills and communication, helps maintain a perspective while also serving as a reminder, and builds self-confidence while reinforcing achievement. It is a better strategic tool for self-improvement than the to-do list which merely fills your day with tasks in no particular order of priority.

Chapter 18:

Time Management

Be not afraid of growing slowly, be afraid only of standing still. – Chinese Proverb

The simple way to teach time management to early teens is to start when they are younger, make it fun, and help them arrange their daily priorities when they may not even know the meaning of this word, so—what's first, next, and last? A small reward will motivate them to follow the plan, and make sure you schedule plenty of free time. Use a calendar or planner and make it colorful. Help them get a sense of time by doing short countdowns—for example when there are five minutes left between playtime and the next activity. Creating a family calendar will help them see how you use time and appreciate how a schedule helps to manage your day or week.

Role Model Time Management

Parents are a child's early role models. If you are always procrastinating, late, and missing deadlines you may find it difficult to convince your teen to be a model of efficiency. School Days are pretty much structured. Co-curricular activities and extra-curricular activities plus homework and assignments can fill up their week. Teens look to the weekend to sleep in late after a stressful week. While many parents indulge their teens by letting them sleep till late morning on weekends, researchers say this can cause their body clock to be out of step with external time as they tend to sleep later too. Waking up at 6 a.m. on a Monday morning could cause them to feel jet lagged because the body clock may be reading 1 am. This makes it difficult for your teen to concentrate at school. When this happens regularly it can influence your teen's mood too. Still, you may want to indulge your teen with an extra hour or two of sleep during the weekend. But set an alarm, open up the curtains or schedule an activity to wake them up.

Everyone's Body Clock Works Differently

Whether your teen is an early bird or a night owl, show them how a simple hack can enlist their brain to work while they sleep, helping them to be better prepared for the next day. Well into the middle of the last century science believed that both the body and the brain were dormant during sleep. Latter-day research has established that the brain is actually at work while we sleep processing and making sense of the day's events as well as doing housekeeping by cleaning out toxins or waste from brain cells. Making a to-do list and spending five to ten minutes before they sleep discussing how they might approach doing the most important tasks helps the mind sort through and process the alternatives while they sleep. They wake up feeling better prepared to take on the day and possibly even with a new idea they have not considered before.

Sharing Schedules Helps Build the Habit

If you are a single parent or a working mom, involving your teen when you plan out your work schedule for the day helps reassure them because they know where you are and are interested in the work you do. When your work takes you away from home, your travel itinerary can be shared well ahead of your trip. Firstly, it gives your teen time to get adjusted to the fact that you are away from them for a few days and more importantly together you can plan for their activities during that time. That helps you too since your mind is at ease knowing what they may be doing in your absence but more importantly, arrange backup for them from extended family, friends or neighbors should they too have co-curricular or extra-curricular activity during the time you are away. Parents should start this during the toddler and pre-teen years, and they will find that their teen adopts time management and scheduling their activities almost seamlessly as they grow older. Seeing how you handle conflicting schedules and negotiating workloads help them in developing the confidence to do this themselves. Having a mom that contributes to the family economy sets a good example of shared responsibility and reassures children of a level of stability should one parent lose their job, as is currently happening worldwide as a fallout from the pandemic and the inflation-recession cycle.

Chapter 19:

Money Matters

I'd like to live as a poor man with lots of money. –Pablo Picasso

Money can't buy happiness, but it will certainly provide for your basic needs—food, clothing, shelter, and pay for healthcare when you need it. Perversely though, money is also the leading cause of bad stress which can lead to ill health. Seventy-two percent of Americans reported feeling stressed about money in a 2015 survey on Stress In America conducted by the American Psychological Association. So, it makes sense to be more mindful of money.

But first, we should recognize that the very nature of money is changing, and future generations may not even see it in the form their parents used, which is "fiat" money—notes and coins which exist by government order as a medium of exchange, and as balances in checkable deposits, cashable through checks and debit cards. Fiat money became popular quite rapidly since its first use in China in the 10th. Century because it was convenient to use as a unit of account too, as opposed to previous stores of value like gold.

Money Is Moving From Digital to Virtual for Teens

Around the time that your Alpha Gen early teen was born (2009), the first digital currencies emerged. In any case, by this time electronic transfers and credit cards had begun to reduce the use of physical currencies. But this required third-party verification and maintaining these financial networks is expensive. Cryptocurrency eliminates this requirement because the blockchain technology on which it is based is an automated mechanism that authenticates transactions and records data in a form that cannot be changed. Transactions in crypto have a high level of confidentiality but since not everyone is a software engineer, most users need to use an exchange to store and transact. Crypto is still quite unstable but enthusiasts point to the fact that it steadily rises in value. A crypto exchange is similar to the stock market with prices fluctuating based on whether crypto bulls or bears are dominant on the day. Unlike stock markets which have fixed hours of operation, crypto can be traded 24-7, 365.

The biggest drawback to cryptocurrencies is hackers, the modern version of bank robbers, and unregulated exchanges–potentially the modern robber barons. The lack of integrity of operators of exchange, through which you trade and store your crypto coins, have been highlighted with the recent bankruptcy of FTX in which $33 Bn was stored and siphoned off through loans to Alameda Research a small trading firm set up by the FTX founder.

Teach Them How to Use Money to Create Wealth

Your teen needs to know that there are basically five ways the money could be used. Money can be used for living expenses, donated, used to pay off debt, saved, or grown. Money saved or grown can be used to create a reservoir of wealth in the form of assets. Assets are usually held in the form of property, stocks, fixed-income deposits, or mutual funds. Less popular, but potentially valuable forms are gold and precious metals, diamonds and precious stones, art, and collectibles. A motorcar too could be an asset because it can be sold fairly quickly but repairs and maintenance costs make it a depreciating asset. A useful metaphor to explain the difference between money (or cash) and assets is to compare cash with water in a hydroelectric dam. It generates power as it flows out and the water level keeps dropping until it is restored by new water in the form of rain. An asset, on the other hand, works for you even when you are sleeping. It is like a spring fed by an underground aquifer—it never dries up.

A practical way to demonstrate wealth creation is through compound interest versus simple interest. Compound interest earns interest on interest and is one of the best ways to build a fund for a long-term goal like college, buying a house, or early retirement. You may be able to demonstrate the difference by putting in some money for your teen in two savings accounts—one in which they get a fixed interest paid at the end of 12 months and the other should have interest compounded monthly (some banks have teen checking accounts that credit interest monthly). If both accounts have the same rate of interest, the second account will have more. Many banks also have digital accounts that offer a mix of fixed interest and mutual funds for teen savers, but you need to be wary of fees.

In today's knowledge economy digital assets have emerged as a new avenue of wealth creation.

Chapter 20:

Transportation And Travel

We don't always know how to get along with her, but you certainly can't get along without her. And if that isn't marriage, I certainly don't know what is. –Groucho Marx, Merrily We Roll Along, 1961.

The invention of the internal combustion engine changed the world. It democratized transportation—cars, buses, motorbikes, and Uber on land, air travel, ships, and submarines on the seas created unimaginable wealth for oil-producing nations. Groucho Marx is credited with planting the seed of the story of America's love affair with cars with the quotation above, in a TV program "The DuPont Show Of The Week, when DuPont was a 23% shareholder in General Motors in 1961 (The Washington Post, n.d.)

But will the internal combustion engine survive the global push for net carbon zero emissions that are dominating today's climate change conversation? Fossil fuels and coal are the top targets for climate change activists in their campaign to slow global warming. Europe and the United States plan to phase out new petrol and diesel vehicles in 15 years *(when your early teen will be 25)*. Car buyers in China are already buying more plug-in vehicles than in the rest of the world. In Norway, more than 60% of new cars registered in 2020 were electric. The electricity for this new breed of vehicles will come from renewable sources like wind, solar, tidal, and biogas, as well as hydrogen and nuclear. While greenhouse gasses reduce, the question of toxic waste from the millions of batteries needing disposal when their lifespan ends is an issue that will occupy the minds of policymakers and environmentalists alike.

This new breed of vehicle is driven by technology that is different from what millennial parents experienced when they took their first steps in learning to drive by backing the family car in and out of their parent's driveway. The new generation of cars that your Alpha Teen will drive will need less maintenance but will have more technology to make driving less stressful and more enjoyable.

Travel Broadens the Mind but Kills the Environment

Extraterrestrial travel, science fiction when millennials were teenagers, is becoming a reality too. But, as space travel grows, the polluting effects of space rockets are also increasingly under scrutiny. Previously there were too few space flights to be able to measure their impact on the environment although the carcinogenic effects of UDMH rocket fuel in pioneering Soviet-era space flight is well documented and visible in the ravaged Kazakh Steppe, the home of the first Cosmodrome. As commercial and scientific rocket launches increase in number safer propellants are in use but there is concern about the black soot generated right through the layers of the atmosphere to the outer mesosphere where it lasts much longer than in the lower levels.

Augmented Reality Is Changing the Way Travel Is Experienced

Electric cars have a simpler technology with fewer mechanical parts and with fewer breakdowns, requiring less maintenance. Multi-point car inspections will become history. The automobile industry is rapidly embracing Augmented Reality

(AR). While it may not completely replace car dealerships in the future, it will allow them to broaden their reach and provide prospective buyers with an online experience. This makes it easier for buyers to shop around and check out car performance and deals without having to visit multiple showrooms. Buyers can also personalize their car by trying out options without having to deal with the high-pressure salesmanship that is the hallmark of the vehicle industry. Some dealerships are planning to experiment with a total online sales model which could drive down inventory costs while others are using AR to transform the in-store experience.

Because the automobile industry plays a significant role in both economic growth and society, competition amongst automakers is intense with new models, features and benefits rolled out annually. Incorporating AR inside the vehicle is thus being seen by them as a source of competitive advantage. Traditional instrumentation is being replaced by visual information projecting traffic and environment conditions and navigation, on the windscreen. The thick, complex paper-based instruction manual that accompanies every car is being replaced by AR tutorials and guidance. Even in traditional service centers, AR is being used for the training of staff and vehicle inspection.

While the shift to electric makes the mechanics simpler, new-generation automobiles could be packed with more technology. Sonar, radar systems, and navigation aids connected through mobile networks will be guiding autonomous vehicles. Though only Tesla and Waymo from Google are currently testing self-driving cars, major car manufacturers like Mercedes Benz, Volkswagen, and Chrysler have semi-autonomous vehicles on sale and are working towards fully autonomous driving in the near future. Your teen will be able to hop into their car and be driven directly to the office without having to give the car any instructions if that's their weekday routine. The car can then drive itself back home till it is needed again to save on parking fees, or it can drive around the city as a ride-hailing service vehicle to earn your teen extra money. It can drop off laundry or pick up groceries too on its way. Autonomous cars do not commit traffic offenses which are good news for their owners but bad news for police departments which in some US states generate 100% of their income from traffic offenses. If the technology driving autonomous vehicles is overwhelming to you, remember that your teen, unlike your generation, is born into technology, has grown up in an interactive world, and is extremely comfortable communicating through VR or AR headsets.

Will Your Teen Need a Driving License?

So, does this mean your teen will not need a driving license? Not so fast, because current regulations require a passenger to have one in case of an emergency requiring human intervention. California, considered a bellwether state for Federal legislation, did pass a law in 2016 which said that self-driving cars will not require a driving license. However, this is yet to be followed nationwide and another good reason for a young adult to get one while still possible is that a driving license is a valid voter identification. Also, the back seat of a car is a popular dating site for young teens so learning to drive is almost a teen rite of passage. Don't expect them to find the time to maintain your car for you though. All they need to know for now is how to drive safely, and the prescribed limits for drinking and driving–a pint of beer or a small glass of wine.

Children are generally happy to join in when you are washing and valeting the car. Encourage them to do so, and use this as an opportunity to show them what's under the hood, locations for the tire kit, spare tire, maintenance basics such as tire pressure, oil level gauges, fuel tank indicator, engine, and driving indicators on the instrumentation panel. Your teen will gradually show interest in learning the art of driving.

Chapter 21:

Navigating Life

Introduce your teen to traffic, road, and directional signs by making it a fun activity you share with them while driving, similar to a game of "I spy with my little eye." This will help them recognize and identify them later if they need a driving license test. Pedestrian crossings, traffic stops, filtering onto a main highway or road, and right of way when turning in or out of a minor road should be explained later when your teen shows more interest in learning to drive.

Technology Is Your Teens Compass

Online navigation aids like Google maps and Waze have all but made paper maps redundant. Your tech-savvy teen will be only too happy to be your navigator when needed instead of depending on you to teach them to find the fastest route through road traffic. Train trips through crowded metro stations and bus rides could be more challenging especially if you have to transit across multi-colored metro lines. Especially if the trains or buses themselves are crowded, learning to be alert for the right stop is essential learning. A tap-and-go smart card is useful for replacing the hassle of managing banknotes and coins and is easily recharged through online or digital banking. A ride-hailing app like Uber is safe and convenient to use and your teen may also like its food delivery service—Uber Eats, although DoorDash and GrubHub are more popular as standalone food delivery services. Location sharing on Google maps and WhatsApp are very simple tools for guiding your teen and you to a meeting location. Activating "find my phone" and "find my device" tracks a lost or stolen mobile phone or laptop.

Teach Survival Skills by Disconnecting From the Grid

Packing for a trip—irrespective of the mode of travel is a skill too. While traveling light is an ideal to strive for, this may not be practical on every trip. Vacation homes, apartments, and AirBnB offer comfort and modern conveniences outside of hotel stay that simplifies your holiday travel but moving outside your comfort zone is good for sensitizing your teen to life in the rough. For example, if you are planning a holiday in a remote but idyllic off-grid location then you need to plan your meals well in advance, do your grocery shopping and maybe even pre-cook and freeze your proteins. Standby power for lighting and recharging phones, as well as old-fashioned matches and wax candles, water and snacks for an unforeseen emergency, and toiletries and light clothing for unscheduled stops along the way make holiday packing an art that you should pass on to your teens. It will help them be more resourceful and self-reliant when they venture out on their own as young adults.

Chapter 22:

Earning a Living

The only thing we know about the future is that it will be different. –
Peter Drucker

Peter Drucker's prediction famously became a reality for millennials. The first millennials were in their early teens when the internet was becoming popular in homes and Google search was launched. For their parents, Generation Xers, personal computers, email, and the telephone were the defining technology. millennials grew up with mobile phones and texting and when the first iPhone was launched, the last of the millennial Generation were in their early teens. They rapidly adapted to social media and smart devices which arrived just as their children, the Alpha Generation was born. Gen Alpha Teens are growing up with Virtual Reality (VR) and AR, which are poised to change the way they live and work.

Video games and eSports have already changed the way they play and learn. Virtual gaming has positive influences on teens—improving attention, perception and memory, hand-eye coordination, quick decision-making, and strategic games can improve problem-solving skills. The negative impact of video games is that violent games increase aggressive behavior and addiction to gaming can lead to poor academic performance. Reduced physical activity and snacking instead of eating regular meals can also lead to obesity.

When the Alpha Generation enters the workforce, they would have spent more time learning and Artificial Intelligence(AI) and Robotics technology are predicted to make jobs that are routine, structured, and repetitive redundant.

Routine Jobs Could Be Taken Over by Robot Workers

Any task that is repetitive and structured can be performed more reliably and at a lower cost by robots. AI and Natural Language Processing (NLP) have the potential to change the world of work in ways we cannot still imagine but at their current stage of development are expected to replace humans in many labor-intensive areas, at least in developed economies. In the developing world, we may still see them persist till investments in mobile technology provide the scale and coverage needed. This could happen faster than expected as Low Earth Orbit (LEO) satellites like Elon Musk's StarLink and Google's LEAF replace expensive land-based towers and base stations and underwater cables linking continents. The categories of jobs currently seen as the low-hanging fruit for replacement are:

assembly line and factory workers

cashiers and tellers

bookkeepers

proofreaders

drivers

packing, delivery, and warehousing

telemarketers

journalists

flight engineers

information analysts and researchers

paralegals

credit analysts

receptionists, clerks, cooks, and bartenders

customer service agents

pharmacists

stock traders

referees and umpires

street vendors

soldiers

security guards

Jobs Currently Considered Irreplaceable in the Knowledge Economy

software developers

data scientists

data security specialists

ecommerce experts

digital marketing experts

AI experts

social network experts

HR managers, public relations specialists, planners

creatives and graphic designers

teachers

scientists

psychologists, psychiatrists, therapists

surgeons

sportsmen and sportswomen

content writers

digital content creators

musical artists

lawyers

pilots

Robotics got a boost during the coronavirus pandemic as machines filled the gaps vacated by humans. Though computerized machines and bots can replicate human work they lack the ability to understand emotions and cognitive tasks. Humans are still good at work which requires intellect, creativity, innovation, and compassion.

Conclusion

Whether you think you can or you think you can't, you are right. –Henry Ford

The zero to three years have long been recognized as the most consequential for a child because this is when cognitive development peaks. They can also be the most difficult for parents because as their independence grows and they start to explore mothers have to keep a closer eye on them. As they grow older, they may imitate adult behavior more closely. While this may be seen as following you around and being a little helper in household chores, their brains are like sponges soaking up your values, your attitude to life, and your behavior. These experiences and emotions are stored in their subconscious mind throughout childhood and are influential in forming the beliefs that drive them as they grow older and become parents themselves.

It is only in recent times that researchers have identified that during adolescent years, starting at around 11 years, the brain undergoes another stage of development that heightens emotions to take priority over logical thinking, which develops at a slower pace and is not completed till the early 20s. But this is happening at a time when parents are less likely to be hovering around them since physical development, awareness, and communication skills are well developed at this age. The adolescent teen is thus left isolated to work things out on their own. This is also the toughest age for a child to deal with the separation or divorce of parents.

In my own experience, during an otherwise traumatic childhood, I was fortunate to be touched by love and kindness during both of these most critical times in my life. As an infant, my grandmother gave me shelter and encouraged me to develop my talent in singing and public speaking, and then, Maddy saw me as a pre-teen that needed help and took me under her caregiving mental and emotional stability to progress my education and build a career.

In every sad, distressed, and angry teen that comes to me, I see a reflection of what my life could have been, and I focus my mind to listen to them as individual stories while working with them to identify the outdated and self-limiting beliefs that hold them back. Replacing self-limiting beliefs with a growth mindset takes time. When beliefs are reinforced by parental ignorance or time-pressured responses in the home this becomes even more difficult. Hence my passion to write this book as a guide for busy parents as well as teens who are willing to own the responsibility to improve their lives. I am concerned that the Alpha Generation, already isolated by screens, will further withdraw under the stress of hormonal changes, adolescent growth and peer influence resulting in even poorer mental health than we are now seeing in our schools post-COVID-19 shutdowns.

An Appeal to Busy Parents and Early Teens

The Alpha generation born into a world where technology is omnipresent is growing up to be more visually driven while their millennial parents are likely to be conditioned by texting. This makes the generation gap more complex because visual reactions are quicker and more emotional while the text is more considered and logical. My plea to such parents is to bring back the fun into your life and home.

Use this book as a guide to be open to everyday conversations and activities that lay the foundation for laddering up skills and confidence from the pre-teen years as your child advances to early teens, late teens, and young adults.

Role Model the Values and Behavior You Expect

In the 938 weeks that your child is in your care and before they are ready to leave home at 18 years, parenting this generation means you should be ready to change your role and your parenting style many times as the child develops:

- Playmate

- Pre-teen Advisor

- Early Teen

In previous generations parents had older children helping out but with the trend of marrying later and dual incomes or single parents, the Alpha teen is more likely to be an only child. With no one to turn to in the home, they will be vulnerable to peer influence which can be good or bad depending on the circle of family, friends, neighbors, coaches, collaborators, and spiritual guides that you have developed as your support network. They will then post hoc rationalize their behavior based on the values and beliefs picked up in the home.

The Education System Is Built for Equality Not Equity

Some parents think that the solution lies in schools. Hence the rush to enter children into oversubscribed secondary schools is based on the misguided view that the end product of education is both good examination grades and a socially adjusted and self-confident teenager.

There has in recent times been a move to recognize that all children are not equal. Not because race, class or geography have made them less intelligent but simply because they are disadvantaged by economic or family circumstances that leave them confused and helpless. Absentee parenting deprives children of boundary setting and they are not used to being told what to do. They therefore rebel at rules and direction. Their behavior disrupts classroom learning when they play up to get the attention that they may be missing at home. Some students come to school hungry and are fed by their teachers.

Enlightened teachers, like me, are open to giving such children multiple chances to level up with their more fortunate peers. But in general, the foundation of the comprehensive education system is based on the principle of equality for all. It is a "no excuses" approach based on the idea that exceptions lead to taking advantage of the system. Moving from equality to equity and fairness for all is a great idea. However, what we do in school can be undone at home and the teen then fails to benefit from our dedication, extra chances, extra effort, resources, and time. Eventually, they may spend so much time being disciplined that they fall back academically to the point of no return.

Putting more resources might help children in deprived areas but does not remove the responsibility of parents to break the mold in which they themselves were formed and step up to modeling the habits and behavior they now know their teens will need to develop to succeed in the Web 3.0 world where creativity, problem-solving, critical thinking, motivation, and empathy become the essential skills that open the door to opportunity.

In my next book, I plan to explore the tools and hacks that develop these skills at a leadership level as the Alpha Teen prepares to enter tertiary or vocational education.

References

Account, S. (2017, June 12). Heaven: Answering Kids' Questions. Focus on the Family. https://www.focusonthefamily.com/parenting/heaven-answering-kids-questions/

admin. (2022a, April 27). The Powerful Meaning of Play. Bonnie Harris | Connective Parenting. https://bonnieharris.com/the-powerful-meaning-of-play/

admin. (2022b, October 31). Why Vacationing with Kids Boosts Their Development. Bonnie Harris | Connective Parenting. https://bonnieharris.com/why-vacationing-with-kids-boosts-their-development/

Almond, P. C. (2021, April 16). *Friday essay: what do the 5 great religions say about the existence of the soul?* The Conversation. https://theconversation.com/friday-essay-what-do-the-5-great-religions-say-about-the-existence-of-the-soul-156205

Battling obesity — and telling bullies to "Kiss It!" (n.d.). Www.cnn.com. https://edition.cnn.com/interactive/2022/10/health/obesity-kiss-it-wellness-cnnphotos/

BBC News. (2022, May 25). *America's Gun Culture in 10 Charts.* BBC News. https://www.bbc.com/news/world-us-canada-41488081

Best Time-Management Apps for Students. (2018, January 10). Top Universities.

https://www.topuniversities.com/blog/best-time-management-apps-students

Carter, C. M. (n.d.). The Complete Guide To Generation Alpha, The Children Of Millennials. Forbes. Retrieved November 27, 2022, from https://www.forbes.com/sites/christinecarter/2016/12/21/the-complete-guide-to-generation-alpha-the-children-of-millennials/?sh=106477f43623

Childhood obesity foundation. (n.d.). Are you a "tiger" or a "jellyfish" when it comes to parenting? – Generation Health. Retrieved November 27, 2022, from https://generationhealth.ca/tiger-or-jellyfish-parenting/

Children's and young people's experiences of loneliness - Office for National Statistics. (2018). Ons.gov.uk. https://www.ons.gov.uk/peoplepopulationandcommunity/wellbeing/articles/childrensandyoungpeoplesexperiencesofloneliness/2018

Comaford, C. (n.d.). Got Inner Peace? 5 Ways To Get It NOW. Forbes. Retrieved November 27, 2022, from https://www.forbes.com/sites/christinecomaford/2012/04/04/got-inner-peace-5-ways-to-get-it-now/?sh=520988806672

Communication and the Teenage Brain. | Martyn Richards | TEDxNorwichED. (n.d.). Www.youtube.com. https://www.youtube.com/watch?v=BbruY110Ql8

Contributor, M. M. B. (n.d.). *I talked to 70 parents who raised highly successful adults—here's the "rare" skill they all taught their kids.* CNBC. https://www.cnbc.com/2022/11/05/i-talked-to-70-parents-who-raised-highly-successful-adults-heres-the-rare-skill-they-all-taught-their-kids.html

Crime in England and Wales - Office for National Statistics. (n.d.). Www.ons.gov.uk. Retrieved November 27, 2022, from https://www.ons.gov.uk/peoplepopulationandcommunity/crimeandjustice/bulletins/crimeinenglandandwales/yearendingmarch2022#:

Did several billion people watch the Queen's funeral? (2022, September 20). Full Fact. https://fullfact.org/news/Queen-funeral-viewing-figures/

Driscoll, M. (2019, June 8). All babies are born equal, no matter their race or class. The Telegraph. https://www.telegraph.co.uk/global-health/climate-and-people/babies-born-equal-no-matter-race-class/

DuLong, J. (2022, October 24). *Stop trying to fix yourself, this expert says.* CNN. https://edition.cnn.com/2022/10/24/health/bad-vibes-nora-mcinerny-wellness/index.html

11 Easy Tips to Teach Your Kids Time Management Skills. (n.d.). Verywell Family. https://www.verywellfamily.com/how-to-teach-your-kids-time-management-skills-4126588

explicoblog. (2022, May 26). *Ancient Parenting Tricks That Work.* Explico Blog. https://www.explico.sg/blog/ancient-parenting-tricks-that-work/

Fry, R., & Parker, K. (2018, November 15). *"Post-Millennial" Generation On Track To Be Most Diverse, Best-Educated.* Pew Research Center. https://www.pewresearch.org/social-trends/2018/11/15/early-benchmarks-show-post-millennials-on-track-to-be-most-diverse-best-educated-generation-yet/

Gallo, L. (2022). Speaking of Psychology: The Stress of Money. Apa.org. https://www.apa.org/news/podcasts/speaking-of-psychology/financial-stress

Guarino, B. (2019, March 14). Birth order may not shape personality after all. The Washington Post. https://www.washingtonpost.com/science/2019/03/14/birth-order-doesnt-shape-personality-after-all/

Herrmann. (n.d.). Whole Brain® Thinking | Herrmann. Www.thinkherrmann.com. https://www.thinkherrmann.com/whole-brain-thinking

How to talk to children about shootings. (n.d.). TODAY.com. https://www.today.com/parents/how-talk-children-about-shootings-age-age-guide-t59626

How to Use Harvard Business Review's "Seven Stories" When It Comes to Deciding Thought Leadership Topics. (n.d.). Www.linkedin.com. Retrieved November 27, 2022, from https://www.linkedin.com/pulse/how-use-harvard-business-reviews-seven-stories-when-comes-yogesh-shah?trk=portfolio_article-card_title

In Handwriting vs. Typing Notes, Pen and Paper Might Win Out. (n.d.). Now. Powered by Northrop Grumman. https://now.northropgrumman.com/in-handwriting-vs-typing-notes-pen-and-paper-might-win-out/

Irving, D. (2019). When Do Human Beings Begin? Princeton.edu. https://www.princeton.edu/~prolife/articles/wdhbb.html

Jarrett, C. (2018). How our teenage years shape our personalities. Bbc.com; BBC Future.

https://www.bbc.com/future/article/20180608-how-our-teenage-years-shape-our-personalities

Johns Hopkins Medicine. (2019). *The Science of Sleep: Understanding What Happens When You Sleep*. Johns Hopkins Medicine Health Library. https://www.hopkinsmedicine.org/health/wellness-and-prevention/the-science-of-sleep-understanding-what-happens-when-you-sleep

Karlsson, E. (2019, August 12). *Being left-handed doesn't mean you are right-brained – so what does it mean?* The Conversation. https://theconversation.com/being-left-handed-doesnt-mean-you-are-right-brained-so-what-does-it-mean-121711

Kline, N. (2016). Time to think : listening to ignite the human mind. London Cassell Illustrated.

Kramer, S. (2019, December 12). *U.S. has world's highest rate of children living in single-parent households*. Pew Research Center; Pew Research Center. https://www.pewresearch.org/fact-tank/2019/12/12/u-s-children-more-likely-than-children-in-other-countries-to-live-with-just-one-parent/

Long, C. (2022, February 4). The Great Cursive Writing Debate | NEA. Www.nea.org. https://www.nea.org/advocating-for-change/new-from-nea/great-cursive-writing-debate

Luppi, F. (2016). *When is the Second One Coming?* The Effect of a Couple's Subjective Well-Being Following the Onset of Parenthood. European Journal of Population, 32(3), 421–444. https://doi.org/10.1007/s10680-016-9388-y

McCrindle, M., & Fell, A. (2020). GENERATION ALPHA. https://generationalpha.com/wp-content/uploads/2020/02/Understanding-Generation-Alpha-McCrindle.pdf

McQuenzie, L. (2020, May 29). How Do Fashion Trends Affect Teens? Catwalk Yourself. http://www.catwalkyourself.com/fashion-news/how-do-fashion-trends-affect-teens/

Millennials Are Raising Gen Alpha—Here's The Basic Facts About These Parents. (n.d.). YPulse. Retrieved November 27, 2022, from https://www.ypulse.com/article/2022/10/24/millennial-are-raising-gen-alpha-heres-the-basic-facts-about-these-parents/

Murdock, A. (2017, December 12). The evolutionary advantage of the teenage brain. University of California. https://www.universityofcalifornia.edu/news/evolutionary-advantage-teenage-brain

Nine Big Changes in Young Teens that You Should Know About. (n.d.). Developmental Science. https://www.developmentalscience.com/blog/2014/02/04/nine-big-changes-in-young-teens-that-you-should-know-about

Normative Sexual Behavior | National Center on the Sexual Behavior of Youth. (n.d.). www.ncsby.org. https://www.ncsby.org/content/normative-sexual-behavior

Paleviciute, R. (2020, May 27). How Sustainable Are Sneakers? The Environmental Impact of Sneaker Production. MAKE FASHION BETTER. https://www.makefashionbetter.com/blog/environmental-impact-of-sneaker-production

Parragon, I., Rowe, F., & Rose, S. (2007). *6 Minute Morning*. Parragon Publishing.

Reynolds, N. (2022, April 11). 12 Things Today's Teens Worry About and How to Help. Raising Teens Today. https://raisingteenstoday.com/things-todays-teens-worry-about/

Rosen, D. (2015, October 30). Why "sleeping in" on weekends isn't good for teens - Harvard Health Blog. Harvard Health Blog. https://www.health.harvard.edu/blog/why-sleeping-in-on-weekends-isnt-good-for-teens-201301115763

Sager, J. (2021, August 17). 10 Growth Mindset Strategies to Help Your Students Grow as Learners. Teach Starter. https://www.teachstarter.com/us/blog/growth-mindset-strategies-to-help-your-students-grow-as-learners/

Salamon, M. (2022, November 8). Break free from 3 self-sabotaging ANTs — automatic negative thoughts. Harvard Health. https://www.health.harvard.edu/blog/break-free-from-3-self-sabotaging-ants-automatic-negative-thoughts-202211082847

7 Useful Benefits of Nursery Rhymes. (n.d.). The New Age Parents. https://thenewageparents.com/benefits-of-nursery-rhymes/

Social Media Has Made Teen Friendships More Stressful. (n.d.). Time. https://time.com/6220033/social-media-teen-friendships-stress/

TEDx Talks. (2016). *Religion After Religion: Millennials in a Post-Religious Age* | Paul Robertson | TEDxCSC. On

YouTube. https://www.youtube.com/watch?v=qmLbD3m6Z3w

TEDxSanDiego - Christine Comaford - *Find your Question*. (n.d.). Www.youtube.com. Retrieved November 27, 2022, from https://www.youtube.com/watch?v=Wgc2YMf1Dr0&t=13s

Teenagers Might Have a Problem With Respect But It's Not the One You Think — Developmental Science. (2017, December). Developmental Science. Developmental Science. https://www.developmentalscience.com/blog/2017/11/29/teenagers-might-have-a-problem-with-respect-but-its-not-the-one-you-think

The myth of the American love affair with cars. (n.d.). Washington Post. https://www.washingtonpost.com/news/wonk/wp/2015/01/27/debunking-the-myth-of-the-american-love-affair-with-cars/

The Plot Thins, or Are No Stories New? (2005, April 15). The New York Times. https://www.nytimes.com/2005/04/15/books/the-plot-thins-or-are-no-stories-new.html

The rise of the only child: How America is coming around to the idea of "just one." (2019, June 19). The Washington Post. https://www.washingtonpost.com/lifestyle/on-parenting/the-rise-of-the-only-child-how-america-is-coming-around-to-the-idea-of-just-one/2019/06/19/b4f75480-8eb9-11e9-8f69-a2795fca3343_story.html

The Teenage Brain and its Effects on Behavior. (2011). [YouTube Video]. In YouTube. https://www.youtube.com/watch?v=taId8GDrqRI

The therapeutic power of writing. (n.d.). BBC Bitesize. https://www.bbc.co.uk/bitesize/articles/zbty6v4

United Nations. (n.d.). Www.facebook.com. https://www.facebook.com/unitednations/posts/10000-litres-of-water-are-needed-to-make-a-single-pair-of-jeansby-shopping-secon/10157679840810820/

Vuleta, B. (2021, January 28). Divorce Rate in America: 35 Stunning Stats for 2021. Legaljobs.io. https://legaljobs.io/blog/divorce-rate-in-america/

Watson, S. (2021, September 15). What's that smell? Get rid of body odor. Harvard Health. https://www.health.harvard.edu/staying-healthy/whats-that-smell-common-and-less-common-causes-of-body-odor

Ways to Stay in the Moment. (n.d.). WebMD. Retrieved November 27, 2022, from https://www.webmd.com/balance/features/pay-attention-be-in-the-now

What Do We Call The Generation After Gen-Z? (2019, November 8). HuffPost. https://www.huffpost.com/entry/generation-alpha-after-gen-z_l_5d420ef4e4b0aca341181574

What Teenagers Want You to Know | Roy Petitfils | TEDxVermilionStreet. (2016). [YouTube Video]. On YouTube. https://www.youtube.com/watch?v=fC2z69q3L0o

Why Teenagers Become "Allergic" to Their Parents. (2018, April 11). The New York Times. https://www.nytimes.com/2018/04/11/well/family/why-teenagers-become-allergic-to-their-parents.html

Witherspoon, & Chang, A. (2022, June 28). Tracking where abortion laws stand in every state. The Guardian. https://www.theguardian.com/us-news/ng-interactive/2022/jun/28/tracking-where-abortion-laws-stand-in-every-state

WomensMedia. (n.d.). How Your Subconscious Mind Is Running Your Life And How To Fix It. Forbes. Retrieved November 27, 2022, from https://www.forbes.com/sites/womensmedia/2020/08/03/how-your-subconscious-mind-is-running-your-life-and-how-to-fix-it/?sh=71699c596b07

Writing by Hand Boosts Brain Activity and Fine Motor Skills, Study Shows. (n.d.). Verywell Mind. https://www.verywellmind.com/how-the-dying-art-of-handwriting-boosts-brain-activity-and-fine-motor-skills-5083814

YEC. (n.d.). Council Post: Do College Grades Predict Future Success? Forbes. https://www.forbes.com/sites/theyec/2020/10/19/do-college-grades-predict-future-success/

Tilak, G., Sundke, A., Tilak, M., & Vidyapeeth. (2021). *Impact And Adverse Effects On The Youth Of Crippled Language Used In Social Media Impact And Adverse Effects On The Youth Of Crippled Language Used In Social Media.* Turkish Online Journal of Qualitative Inquiry (TOJQI), 12(6), 4798–4809. http://210.212.169.38/xmlui/bitstream/handle/12345

6789/9982/Turkish%20Journal.pdf?sequence=1&isAllowed=y

"Latchkey Kids": What's Different About Leaving Children Home Alone Now Versus Then. (2017, June 12). HowStuffWorks. https://health.howstuffworks.com/pregnancy-and-parenting/latchkey-kids-children-home-alone-now-then.htm

www.ingramcontent.com/pod-product-compliance
Lightning Source LLC
Chambersburg PA
CBHW042126100526
44587CB00026B/4193